Traditional Home Cooking

Madame Benoit

ISBN: 2-7625-5971-5   Printed in Canada

LES ÉDITIONS HÉRITAGE INC.
300, Arran, Saint-Lambert, Québec J4R 1K5
(514) 875-0327

Cover design: Design Express
Photography: Paul Casavant

I had been married to Jehane Benoit for more than 42 years when she died on Nov. 24th, 1987. I never stressed the letter "H" in her name because I thought of it as part of a mute syllable. Radio and television interviewers, however, found it to be a tongue twister and took the habit of calling her quite simply Madame Benoit.

*J*ehane was born in Montreal on the 22nd of March 1904. Her father Alfred Patenaude was a bank manager and later, inventor of a method to learn English using textbooks and gramophone records. It explains why Jehane could switch from French to English with astonishing facility. Her mother, whose maiden name was Marie-Louise Cardinal, belonged to a family of well-to-do bakers. The Patenaudes came from the land and were used to big family meals served on a large table with a certain amount of formality and due appreciation. Jehane often talked of her grandfather Patenaude whom she would describe as more than slightly particular in his choice of foods. His was the earliest influence on her career as her mother did not have a great inclination toward cooking.

Jehane studied at the Sacré-Coeur in Montreal, a French order of nuns whose mother house was in Paris. The curriculum prepared young women for their role in society and for a degree of Bachelor of Arts which could only be obtained after an additional two-year course in France. Her initial stay in the City of Lights developed in her a strong desire to become an actress. Instead, after a hasty return to Canada, she got her parents' consent to go back to Paris and to register at the University La Sorbonne for a course in food chemistry. She had used the food angle to placate her mother and to enthuse her father for whom eating well was a daily obsession. She intended, however, once there, to attend a theatre school. At the Sorbonne, Edouard de Pomiane held the chair of culinary art and science. He was already well known for his scientific approach to a subject which had relied mostly on experience and observation. His personality was such that Jehane found in him an ideal professor who soon made her forget about the theatre school. She stayed on at the university for the four-year course and traveled throughout France and neighbouring countries during the holidays to learn about culinary traditions.

Jehane came back to Montreal in the late 1920s. Shortly thereafter, she started a cooking school where women of all ages could come to her lectures and demonstrations, free to attend or to leave, free as well to pay what they could afford. That type of teaching soon attracted hundreds of students, shall we say, and brought her recognition for imparting new ideas, and a new approach to cooking. She kept the school going until 1939, figuring at that time that close to 7,000 women had attended her lectures.

I met her in August 1940. She was 36, I was 23. I have never felt that difference in age during our long life together as her natural enthusiasm, her youthful confidence in the future and her energy always surpassed mine. Being together was a joy we could not do without. But I was of military age. The war soon separated us. She found a way of crossing to London, England, in the Summer of 1945 while I was still serving in Holland. We were married in the city and borough of Westminster on the 23rd of August 1945. She stayed with me in Holland until demobilization brought us back to Canada in January 1946.

Jehane had abandoned her Montreal apartment to join me overseas. She also had cut short a career that was barely in its early stages. Ten years would elapse before she could climb up the ladder of success again. She had, by that time, gained recognition for her work through radio and television and from her articles in national magazines. Her voice and face were familiar to most Canadian women. In 1962, she joined me in Paris, where I was posted by my employers, and took advantage of our stay of a year to complete her *Encyclopedia of Canadian Cuisine*. We were back in Canada in September 1963. Jehane resumed her busy schedule of writing, lecturing and counseling. We were now living in the mountains of Sutton on a farm where I still raise sheep. The farm, which we named *Noirmouton*, became the centre of her professional life inasmuch as press, radio, television and business people often came here and sat at her table for a meal or a high tea. The 1970s was the decade during which she wrote most of the 20 odd books which make up her lasting contribution to the art and science of cooking.

Jehane was recommended for the Order of Canada to which she was admitted as an Officer on the 19th of June, 1973. She was nearly 70 years old. The age of technology was suddenly thrust upon the unwitting housewife in the form of the microwave oven. Jehane saw in it a new source of heat which, like gas and electricity, could be applied to age-old recipes in a manner which would bring greater freedom to women. She devoted the years between 1975 and 1987 to the microwave evolution, criss-crossing Canada as its apostle up to the last weeks of her life. It was indeed missionary work. Jehane had time, through it all, to write the *Encyclopedia of Microwave Cooking* which was published in the Fall of 1985. That last piece of work would ensure her place, she thought, in the history of cooking until, at least, man could tame heat from a source yet unknown.

B. Benoit

Noirmouton

CONTENTS

Meats

MEATS

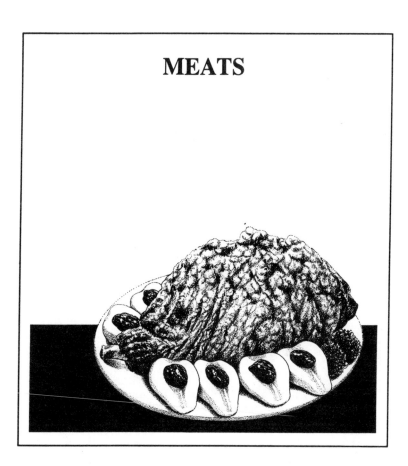

INTRODUCTION

There is a grade of meat for every purpose and a cut to fit every budget.

There is nothing really complex about learning how to buy meat since the various cuts bear an orderly relationship to each other and to the section of the animal from which derive. For example: a loin pork chop is similar to a sirloin or porterhouse steak; both are cut from the middle section of the hind quarter; and both have a fair amount of tenderloin. Keeping these facts in mind for all cuts, it should become easy for you to relate the cut required by the recipe to what is seen on the meat counter.

FOUR WAYS TO TENDERIZE MEAT

Inexpensive, tasty, economical cuts of meat, such as blade and chuck roasts and steaks, stewing beef, pork shoulder, pork liver, etc., can be fork tender by applying one of the following methods:

1. Pound thin slices of tough meat with a meat mallet to soften the fibers. Properly done, this corresponds to the "cubing" of steak.
2. Brush thin slices of meat with equal parts of mixed salad oil and lemon juice and let stand at least 30 minutes or overnight.
3. Cover large cuts of meat with buttermilk, refrigerate overnight, then drain.
4. Let meat stand overnight in a marinade made by heating, without boiling, equal parts of red cooking wine and water with 1 sliced peeled onion, 1 peeled section of garlic (optional) and 1 teaspoon (5 mL) of pickling spices per pint (500 mL). Use part or all of this marinade as the liquid in cooking the meat.

CUTS FOR ROASTING

The Standing Rib is the section next to the wing. It is composed of seven to eight ribs; the one referred to as the "prime rib" is cut from the first five ribs and it is the best.

The Wing Roast is cut from the loin section next to the ribs. It is triangular in shape and contains little or no tenderloin.

The Porterhouse or T-Bone Roast is cut from the loin next to the wing. It contains the T-shaped bone and most of the tenderloin or undercut.

The Sirloin Roast is cut from next to the porterhouse. A rolled roast is easier to carve and sometimes more economical but never as tasty and juicy as the prime rib roast.

The Beef Fillet is expensive, tender and considered by many as the very best; it contains some tenderloin. As this cut is usually prepared for steaks, it is advisable to ask the butcher to reserve one.

RULES FOR ROASTING

No matter how perfect and tender the cut of beef you choose, it can be spoiled in the cooking. The most important rule is not to overcook a roast of beef. Fortunately, through traveling, reading and eating, we have all become more aware of the fact a good beef roast is juicier, tastier and more tender when it is not overcooked — pink, which is medium or medium rare, is the perfect choice. The meat thermometer is almost a must, unless you are among the chosen few who can cook a roast of beef to the right degree by smell and touch. With the thermometer inserted into the centre of the meat, not touching fat or bone, you are sure that the result will always be perfect. For pink, read 120°F (50°C) for rare, read 130°F (55°C); for medium, 140°F (60°C). For very well done (if you must), 150°F to 160°F (70°C to 75°C). When done, remove the roast to a warm platter and let it stand 10 to 15 minutes before carving.

Other things to know are:

1. Remove the roast from refrigerator 2 hours before roasting.
2. Never let the roast touch the metal while roasting. Sit on two flat bones, placed in bottom of pan (ask butcher for them), and use afterwards to make consommé.
3. A 5-to-6 pound (2 1/2-to-3 kg) roast needs 2 teaspoons (10 mL) salt, 1/4 teaspoon (1 mL) pepper.
4. On the best cuts of beef for roasting, you can expect 2 large or 3 medium servings from each pound (500 g) of meat.

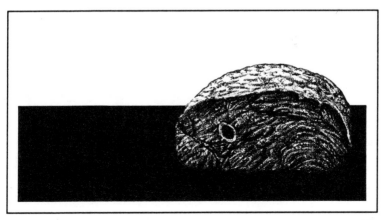

PRIME RIB ROAST OF BEEF

A fine prime rib roast is superb. A standing rib is best if large. Above all, do not have it boned and rolled. Give yourself the luxury of a bone-in prime roast.

3 to 4 ribs of prime of beef
1/4 tsp (1 mL) freshly
  ground pepper

3 tbsp (50 mL) soft butter
1 tbsp (15 mL) dry mustard
2 tsp (10 mL) salt

Score the fat on the top of the roast into diamond shapes. Rub the pepper on the fat. Cream together the soft butter, dry mustard and salt. Spread on the red part of the meat (not on the fat). Place the roast rib-side down in the pan. Roast, uncovered and without basting in a pre-heated 350°F (180°C) oven, 15 minutes per poud (500 g) for rare, 20 minutes per pound (500 g) for medium, or insert thermometer into thickest part of the meat, without touching the bone. Cook according to taste as already explained. When done, place the roast on a hot serving platter, this time resting on its broader flesh side. Allow to stand in warm place 12 to 15 minutes before carving.

To make the gravy, place the roasting pan over direct heat, then choose which one of the three basic gravies you wish to make.

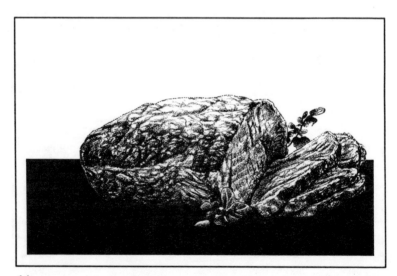

ROAST FILLET OF BEEF

Wing, porterhouse or sirloin roast can be roasted like a prime rib. The beef fillet requires a slightly different treatment.

4 to 6 lb (2 to 3 kg) beef fillet
1 long thin slice of fat, fresh
  or salt pork
3 tbsp (50 mL) butter

1 tbsp (15 mL) dry mustard
salt and pepper
1/2 cup (125 mL)
  diced beef suet

Place the beef fillet on the long thin slice of salted or fresh pork (do not permit the fillet to touch the metal). Salt and pepper to taste. Cream together the butter and the mustard. Butter the beef fillet with it. Top with the diced beef suet. Place in an oven preheated for 15 minutes at 450°F (230°C). Roast 30 to 40 minutes in all until the thermometer registers 120°F to 130°F (50°C to 55°C), according to taste. (The beef fillets vary so much in weight and quality, that only a meat thermometer assures you of a perfect result.)

To make red wine beef fillet, proceed the same way but baste 3 to 4 times with hot red wine during the cooking period.

To serve it cold:

Cook only to rare or medium and let the meat cool in the dripping pan covered with a foil paper. The beef is at its best served at room temperature rather than refrigerated.

THE FINISHING TOUCHES
TO A PERFECT ROAST

Three ways to make gravy

1. A creamy sauce, obtained by the addition of flour.
2. A clear sauce, made by adding a cold liquid to the fat in the pan.
3. The perfect gravy, made by adding a can of cold undiluted consommé to all the very hot fat in the dripping pan. Just heat and serve.

Good flour gravy has an appetizing color. To make it a rich brown, cook the flour in the fat over direct heat until the flour is well browned, which usually takes 5 to 8 minutes cooking.

Whole wheat flour always makes a tastier and browner gravy. But if you use ordinary white flour, it is preferable to brown it in advance, keeping it handy for use when required. To brown flour, simply spread it on a flat pan and heat slowly in a 300°F (150°C) oven, as if you were making Melba toast. Stir it occasionally and keep on cooking until it is light brown. Pass through a sieve to remove all lumps and store in a glass jar in a cold place. The perfect proportions for a flour gravy are 2 tablespoons (30 mL) of fat to 2 tablespoons (30 mL) of flour. If you use more than 2 tablespoons of fat, the gravy always separates and becomes greasy. Use 1/2 cup (125 mL) of liquid to each tablespoon (15 mL) of flour. (Whole wheat and highly browned flour have less thickening power and it is best to add an extra tablespoon (15 mL) of either one.)

The liquid used to make a clear gravy makes a big difference. It is not a set rule that you must use cold water. Leftover tea or coffee, tomato juice, milk, cream, wine, etc. will give a completely different flavor and color.

Roast Fillet of Beef →

Simplified Brown Sauce

If you like a lot of gravy and use the fat to make the Yorkshire pudding, the English way, make this sauce which is easy to prepare. (Made from classic brown stock, it requires a long and involved preparation.) This sauce will keep 8 to 10 days refrigerated, 3 to 6 months frozen.

1/4 cup (60 mL) minced onion
1/2 tsp (2 mL) sugar
2 tbsp (30 mL) butter
2 tbsp (30 mL) flour
2 cups (500 mL) canned beef
  consommé

1/8 tsp (0,5 mL) pepper
1/4 tsp (1 mL) thyme
1 bay leaf
2 tsp (10 mL) tomato paste

Cook the onion and the sugar in the butter for 5 minutes; stir in the flour and cook over low heat, stirring constantly until browned.

Gradually add the consommé, stirring until it reaches the boiling point. Add the pepper, thyme, bay leaf and tomato paste. Cook over low heat 20 minutes. Strain. Makes 1 1/2 cups (375 mL).

Madeira Sauce

An English favorite and a very elegant sauce.

1/2 cup (125 mL) Madeira or
  port wine
1 recipe simplified
  brown sauce

2 tbsp (30 mL) butter

Boil the Madeira or port until reduced to 3 tablespoons (50 mL).

Add the brown sauce to the reduced wine. Cover and simmer for 5 minutes. Remove from heat, add the butter and stir until melted. Serve.

← *Potage St. Germain*
← *My Lentil Soup*

Sauce Robert

The classic sauce of French Cuisine, used to reheat quickly thinly sliced leftover roast of beef.

1 onion, minced
1 tbsp (15 mL) butter
1 tbsp (15 mL) salad oil
1 cup (250 mL) white wine
1 recipe of simplified
   brown sauce

3 to 4 tsp (15 to 20 mL)
   prepared Dijon mustard
3 tbsp (50 mL) soft butter
3 tbsp (50 mL) parsley,
   minced

Brown the onion in the 1 tablespoon (15 mL) butter and salad oil. Add the wine and boil over high heat until reduced to 3 to 4 tablespoons (50 to 60 mL).

Heat the brown sauce and add the reduced wine. Simmer for a few moments, while stirring.

Blend together the mustard, soft butter and minced parsley. Remove the sauce from the heat and add the mustard mixture. Stir until the butter is dissolved. Taste for seasoning and use.

YORKSHIRE PUDDING

There is the Canadian type and the English type of Yorkshire; both are good and so the choice is a matter of taste.

Canadian Yorkshire Pudding

3 eggs
1 cup (250 mL) milk
3 tbsp (50 mL) melted butter

1 cup (250 mL) flour
1/2 tsp (2 mL) salt

Preheat oven to 375°F (190°C). Grease nine 3-inch (7.5 cm) muffin cups. Beat eggs slightly in the milk and butter. Then gradually beat in flour and salt. Pour 1 teaspoon (5 mL) hot beef fat into each cup. Then fill muffin cups about 3/4 full. Bake 40 minutes or until light to lift and golden brown. Remove from oven. Serve immediately.

POT ROAST AT ITS BEST

Some of the more common and likely to be available cuts for braising or pot roasting are the following:

1. **Boneless brisket**
2. **Cross-cut shanks (very tasty)**
3. **Round bone or trimmed-bone chuck roast**
4. **Short rib or English pot roast**
5. **Sirloin tip**
6. **Standing rump roast**
7. **Rolled rump roast**
8. **Bottom round with bone or boneless**
9. **Heel or round**
10. **Oxtail**
11. **Plate beef with bones or rolled**

Some of these cuts are quite lean, such as the round. Others have varying amounts of fat to enhance the flavor and texture.

Braising the Beef

Brown meat on all sides in its own fat removed from the cut, diced and melted, or use other fat or foil of your choice.

Brown the meat over medium low heat as slow browning gives the best results in color and flavor. The meat can be coated in flour before browning.

When the browning is over, pour off the collected fat if you are counting calories. Then season the meat with salt and pepper; add herbs, onion, garlic or other desired seasoning.

At that point, add a small amount of liquid if you so desire, about 1/4 cup (60 mL) is sufficient for 3 to 5 pounds (1.5 to 2.5 kg) of meat, or no liquid at all. Cover tightly and simmer over very low heat or in a 325°F (165°C) oven until fork tender, which will take from 1 1/2 to 3 hours depending on thickness, quantity and cut of the meat.

When cooked, there will be quite a good quantity of liquid whether some was added or not. According to taste, it can be thickened by adding 1 1/2 tablespoons (22 mL) of flour mixed with a little water to form paste, for each cup (250 mL) of liquid in the pan. Add and simmer while stirring, for a minute or two.

Pot Roasting the Beef

Proceed the same way as for braising in browning and seasoning, then add cold water or another liquid of your choice. Use from 1 to 3 cups (250 to 750 mL) of liquid. Cover tightly and simmer over low heat until fork tender. It takes from 2 to 3 1/2 hours.

POT ROAST BOUQUET

A bouquet of favorite vegetables around the roast gives it its name.

3 to 5 lb (1.5 to 2.5 kg)
  rolled chuck or rump of beef
1 clove garlic, cut in two
2 tsp (10 mL) salt
3 tbsp (50 mL) flour
2 tbsp (30 mL) fat of your
  choice

1 cup (250 mL) water
1/2 tsp (2 mL) thyme or
  marjoram
6 medium potatoes, peeled
6 to 8 medium carrots,
  grated
6 medium onions, peeled

Rub the meat all over with the cut clove of garlic. Sprinkle with the salt, then rub in the flour.

Brown the meat on all sides in fat, over medium low heat, then place meat on a flat rack, placed in the bottom of the pan. Add water and thyme or marjoram. Cover tightly. Simmer over low heat or bake in 350°F (180°C) oven for 1 hour per pound (500 g).

Add the vegetables around the meat in the last hour of cooking.

According to taste, thicken the gravy with flour mixed in cold water. Taste for seasoning. Serves 6.

As a variation: When adding the vegetables, add 1 1/4 cups (315mL) chili sauce, 2 medium onions chopped fine, 1tsp (5mL) dill seeds or curry powder.

MY FAVORITE POT ROAST

Lots of flavor with a tantalizing aroma as it cooks.

3 to 4 lb (1.5 to 2 kg) round
  bone chuck roast or bottom
  round
2 tbsp (30 mL) soft butter or
  olive oil
2 tsp (10 mL) salt
1/4 tsp (1 mL) freshly
  ground pepper

1 large unpeeled lemon,
  sliced
2 medium onions, thinly
  sliced
1 cup (250 mL) ketchup
1/2 tsp (2 mL) tarragon or
  basil
1/4 cup (60 mL) red wine or
  water

Place meat in a large baking dish. Rub top with softened butter or with oil. Season with salt and pepper. Cover with slices of lemon and onion. Combine remaining ingredients and pour over meat.

Cover tightly so the meat will steam tender.
Cook in a 350°F (180°C) oven for 2 to 3 hours or until tender. Serves 6.

POT-AU-FEU

Pot-au-feu (or boiled beef) means a kind of homemade family soup simmered in a deep earthenware pot; essentially, it is a complete meal, composed of different meats and birds, lots of ''pot vegetables'' and subtle flavoring. It is regarded as one of the oldest cooking methods and is a traditional family meal; as such, it has all types of variations, and it is served around the world.

3 to 5 lb (1.5 to 2.5 kg) meatless beef bones
2 1/2 lb (1.2 kg) brisket, shank, cross-cut, round or chuck
1 lb (500 g) chicken giblets
4 qts (4 L) cold water
1 tbsp (15 mL) coarse salt
4 onions, left whole

4 carrots, left whole
1 or 2 leeks, split in half (if available)
1 cup (250 mL) diced celery and leaves
4 whole cloves
1 tsp (5 mL) thyme
1/2 tsp (2 mL) dry mustard

Ask the butcher to crack or cut the bones. Place in a large soup kettle, add the meat and the cleaned chicken giblets. Pour the cold water over all. Add the salt. Cover and bring to the boiling point over medium heat. When it boils, remove the grey scum that accumulates on top with a perforated spoon. Then add remaining ingredients, again bring back to the boiling point and skim with the perforated spoon. Cover and simmer over low heat 3 to 4 hours or until the beef is tender. Remove the meat and vegetables. Serves 6-8.

PETITE MARMITE

Called Petite (or Little) Marmite, it is the grandest and most elegant of all pot-au-feu. Many chic and exclusive Parisian restaurants feature it as a specialty. Traditionally, it is cooked and served in a special deep earthenware pot. However, any saucepan will do to cook it.

3/4 lb (350 g) top round	3 sets of chicken giblets
1 lb (500 g) rib of beef	2 leeks or 4 onions
1 large marrow bone, sliced	3 carrots, whole
10 cups (2.5 L) cold beef or	1 small head of celery, cut in 4
chicken broth	1 small cabbage, cut in wedges

Wrap the round and rib of beef and the marrow bone in a cheesecloth. Place in saucepan with the cold beef broth. Bring to a rolling boil and skim.

Add the chicken giblets, the leeks split in two (the green and the white) or the whole onions, the carrots, celery and cabbage. Bring back to a boil. Cover and simmer over very low heat for 4 hours. Taste for seasoning.

To serve, remove surplus fat. Unwrap the meat on a hot dish. Remove the marrow from the bones, cut the meat into individual portions.

Prepare 6 slices of toasted bread, set one per plate, spread each one with marrow and pour some of the broth on top. Then serve a helping of meat and vegetables on top of each. Serves 6.

Green Sauce

A classic sauce to serve with all types of pot-au-feu, especially the Petite Marmite. Will keep 6 to 8 weeks, refrigerated, covered. Leave at room temperature for a few hours before serving as the oil will cloud when refrigerated.

1 small onion, grated	1 tbsp (15 mL) coarse
3 tbsp (50 mL) parsley,	breadcrumbs
chopped	4 tbsp (60 mL) salad oil
1 tbsp (15 mL) capers,	juice of 1/2 a lemon
chopped	salt and pepper to taste
1 clove garlic, crushed	

Place in a bowl the onion, parsley, capers, garlic and breadcrumbs. Mash together until well blended. Add the oil and lemon juice gradually, stirring all the time until well blended. Salt and pepper to taste. Yield: about 1 cup (250 mL).

GREAT STEAKS

WORLD FAMOUS STEAK AU POIVRE

Men seem to have a real fondness for this biting steak.

**2 lb (1 kg) sirloin or T-Bone
steak, 1 1/2-inch (3.5-cm)
    thick
3/4 tsp (3 mL) coarse ground
    peppercorns
1/2 tbsp (7 mL) coarse salt**

**2 tbsp (30 mL) butter
2 tbsp (30 mL) salad oil
1/4 cup (60 mL) consommé*
1/2 cup (125 mL) red wine or
    brandy**

Place half the pepper and half the coarse salt on top of the steak and pound in lightly with the back of a wooden spoon. Turn and do same on the second side. Let stand at room temperature from 1 to 3 hours.

To cook, heat the butter and salad oil to smoking point in a large heavy metal frying pan. Put in the steak. Sauté over fast heat until seared and browned: 5 minutes on each side for rare, 7 minutes for medium rare. Lower heat slightly, only if necessary, during the cooking period. Place the steak on a heated serving plate. Keep warm. Add the consommé, red wine or brandy to the pan juices, stir while scraping the bottom until it just comes to a boil. Then simmer over low heat 2 minutes. Spoon over the steak. Serve with bunches of watercress, creamed spinach and boiled buttered rice. Serves 4.

*Use undiluted canned consommé.

STEAK MAITRE D'HOTEL

This one hails from Old France, but it has become a classic of the world's cuisine. Simple but delicious.

**1 steak for broiling, cut
    1 1/2-to-2 inches
    (3.5-to-5 cm) thick
4 tbsp (60 mL) soft butter**

**1 tbsp (15 mL) parsley, minced
1/4 tsp (1 mL) dry mustard
1 tsp (5 mL) lemon juice
salt and pepper to taste**

Broil or barbecue steak to the degree of doneness preferred. Salt and pepper. Cream together the butter, mustard, lemon juice and parsley. Shape in little balls or simply place a teaspoon over each portion of steak as soon as served. The butter melts by the heat of the steak and spreads its delicious flavor on top. Serves 4.

DEUTSCHES HAMBURGER

The father of all hamburgers was born in Hamburg, Germany. Many a tourist has been confused when he ordered ''Deutches Beesteak'' and received what he knew as hamburger. The following recipe is the original.

1 lb (500 g) hamburger
1 lb (500 g) lean pork, ground
1 medium onion, quartered
2 tbsp (30 mL) parsley, minced
2 eggs
2 tsp (10 mL) salt

1/2 tsp (2 mL) pepper
pinch of caraway seeds or lemon peel, grated
2 tbsp (30 mL) butter, melted
3 tbsp (50 mL) all purpose flour
2 tbsp (30 mL) butter or fat
2 onions, thinly sliced

Pass the hamburger meat and ground pork through a food grinder along with the onion and the parsley. Add the eggs, salt, pepper, caraway seeds or grated lemon peel, melted butter and flour. Knead with your fingers until the ingredients are thoroughly blended. Shape the meat into 8 patties, then cover and refrigerate 1 to 4 hours.

Heat the butter or fat of your choice in a heavy cast iron frying pan. When the fat is quite hot, add the meat patties and fry on both sides. Remove to a hot platter. Separate the onion slices into rings and add them to the fat remaining in the pan. Sauté a few minutes over highr heat, stirring constantly until the onions are soft and golden brown. Spon over the hamburgers. Serves 6 to 8.

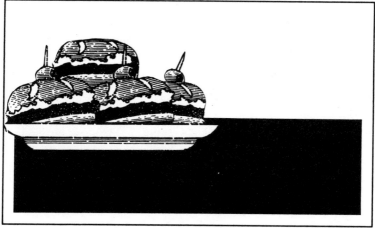

FROM SCALOPPINE TO SCHNITZEL

A veal chop has many names and shapes; each for some reason, once prepared and cooked, tastes quite different. Even people who never eat veal love schnitzel or scaloppine, possibly because of the tenderness and delicate flavor that veal acquires when thinly sliced and cooked in a special way. The important point is to understand the difference between each type of cutlet, then the cooking becomes easy.

French Escalope. The mother of all the others. Escalope means a thin slice of meat flattened slightly and fried in butter. In the old days, the terms was used to describe a dish of any thinly sliced meat; sliced lamb was called **escalope d'agneau**, etc., but nowadays it refers only to veal. Basically it came from the word **collop** or **escaloper**, meaning to cut meat or vegetables into thin slices.

Italian Scaloppine. They are not like the veal cutlets because they are sliced thinly from the leg, then cut again into small squares, and pounded until almost paper thin.

German Schnitzel. Cut and prepared the same way as Italian Scaloppine, or sometimes thinly sliced from the boned loin section, it is also pounded to break the fibers but not to make paper thin. The meat is then breaded and sautéed.

English Collop. Simply a corruption of the French escalope.

Veal, contrary to beef, has no natural fat covering and no marbling of fat inside the meat which is why such thin cuts as scaloppine, escalope, etc., are at their best sautéed, and always at medium to low heat. The best fats to use are: unsalted or salted butter, olive oil, half butter half salad oil, or melted kidney fat, the last giving the best flavor.

FRENCH ESCALOPES

A true French cut is taken from the leg cutting — the meat is cut on the bias, into thin slices, about 1/3-inch (0,8-cm) thick. Each piece should weigh 3 to 4 ounces (85 to 115 g) at most and should be free of fat and gristle. When the veal is young and tender, there is no need to pound it. When in doubt, flatten a little with a rolling pin. Slash the edges so that they will lie flat in cooking.

4 French-cut veal escalopes
3 tbsp (50 mL) unsalted or
salted butter
3 tbsp (50 mL) salad oil
1 tbsp (15 mL) warm water

1 small onion, minced
pinch of tarragon or thyme
4 tbsp (60 mL) rich cream
salt and pepper

Heat the butter and 1 1/2 tablespoons (22 mL) of the oil in a heavy enamel cast iron frying pan. When very hot, brown the escalopes on both sides, turning only once. Season with salt and pepper. Add the warm water, cover and simmer over low heat for 30 minutes, turning two or three times. Meanwhile, heat the rest of the oil in a frying pan, add the onion and fry quickly. At this point, for a nice variation 1/2 lb (227 g) thinly sliced fresh mushrooms can be added to the onion and quickly fried together. Add the tarragon or thyme. Simmer 5 minutes.

When ready to serve, pour onion over veal, add the cream, bring to a quick boil. Taste for seasoning. Serve with sautéed potatoes, beans or carrots. Serves 4.

ITALIAN SCALOPPINE

Each part of Italy has its own way of cooking scaloppine. The following is the Emilia type. Lemon juice and scaloppine are almost inseparable, whichever way they are cooked. They are at their best made with a light Italian olive oil such as Bertholi, but salad oil can be used.

4 veal scaloppine
1 tsp (5 mL) flour
1/4 cup (60 mL) oil or melted
** butter**
juice of 1 lemon

grated rind of 1/2 a lemon
1/4 cup (60 mL) parsley,
** minced**
salt and pepper

Prepare the scaloppine as given in the basic method discussed for Italian Scaloppine. Rub each side with a little flour, using the tips of the fingers. Heat the oil or melt the butter in a heavy enamel cast iron frying pan, brown the meat on both sides, turning only once; it will take about 2 to 3 minutes per side. Then add the lemon juice and rind. Sprinkle with the parsley, salt and pepper. Cover and simmer over low heat for 10 minutes. Serve with fine noodles, tossed with butter and parsley, and a green salad. Serves 4.

GERMAN SCHNITZEL

No cut of meat is more popular in Germany than the Schnitzel. The breaded cutlets sould be allowed to stand at room temperature for 15 to 30 minutes before being fried.

A schnitzel will brown on both sides and thoroughly cook in 8 to 12 minutes, turning only once. If it takes longer, it is because the meat has been cut too thick; it should then be fried and turned once more the same as the first cooking. Schnitzel is best fried in butter, but vegetable shortening or lard can be used.

6 veal escalopes
juice of 1 lemon
1/2 cup (125 mL) flour
2 eggs
2 tbsp (30 mL) cold water

2 tbsp (30 mL) salad oil
1 1/2 cups (375 mL) fine
  breadcrumbs
4 to 5 tbsp (60 to 75 mL)
  butter or shortening

Place the pounded escalopes in a dish, pour the lemon juice on top. Let stand 30 minutes.

Remove from platter, sprinkle with salt on both sides. Set flour on a piece of waxed paper. Beat the eggs lightly with water, then beat in the oil. Pour the breadcrumbs on a flat plate. Dip both sides of each escalope first in flour, then in the beaten eggs and dredge each one with the breadcrumbs. Let stand at room temperature for 15 to 30 minutes.

Heat butter or fat quite hot in a large frying pan. Place the escalopes one next to the other, but do not crowd; do 2 or 3 at a time or as many as you can fit in your large frying pan.

Fry the first side over low heat until there is a golden brown crust. Turn over with spatula (never pierce with a fork). When brown on both sides, which should take from 4 to 6 minutes on each side, they are ready to serve.

To keep warm, place cooked meat on a warm platter or baking sheet in a 250°F (120°C) oven. Serves 6.

SCALOPPINE MILANESE

Famous around the world. Contrary to the Schnitzel, these breaded escaloppine should be coated only when ready to cook. The classic way to serve them is with green peas and rice.

4 veal scaloppine	3 tbsp (50 mL) butter
1 egg beaten	2 tbsp (30 mL) olive oil
1 cup (250 mL) finely sifted	juice of 1/2 a lemon
dry breadcrumbs	1/4 tsp (1 mL) pepper
1/2 tsp (2 mL) salt	

Brush both sides of each scaloppine with the beaten egg. Then sprinkle thoroughly on both sides with the fine breadcrumbs mixed with salt.

Place butter in a large frying pan and melt it. Add the olive oil. When very hot, add the meat and fry golden brown on low heat, turning only once. It takes from 3 to 6 minutes on each side.

Place in a warm dish, sprinkle with the lemon juice and pepper. Serves 4.

SAUSAGES

Sausages are easy on the budget, and well prepared, they are delicious. As they cook quickly and require little attention, they eliminate a lot of hustle-bustle for the mother.

There are four basic methods to cook sausages to perfecion. The all important factor in each one is to cook them over medium and medium-low heat. Never rush the cooking. For drier sausages, remove the fat as it accumulates.

First Method — Pan fried sausages. Place the sausages in a cold frying pan, lightly greased, and cook over medium heat 15 to 20 minutes, turning often until they are browned evenly. Remove excess fat as it collects.

Second Method — To keep the sausages more plump and lean, prick with a fork and pour boiling water over them. Cover and bring to a boil. Drain and fry slowly until browned evenly, following the first method.

Third Method — Baked sausages. Spread the sausages in a lightly greased shallow pan. Bake 25 to 30 minutes in a 350°F (180°C) oven. Turn the sausages once during the baking. This method is a time saver if you are baking something else in the oven at that time.

Fourth Method — Broiled sausages. Place the sausages in the broiler pan 5 to 6 inches (12 to 15 cm) from direct heat and broil 2 to 3 minutes on each side, or until brown.

GREEN GRAPES AND SAUERKRAUT SAUSAGES

A can of sauerkraut, half a pound (250 g) of sausages, and a cup (250 mL) of seedless grapes combined, and you will have a gourmet's treat. All of it will be ready in 25 minutes.

1 28-oz (796 mL) can or
  1 1/2 lb (750 g) sauerkraut
1 large onion, diced
2 tbsp (30 mL) butter

1/2 cup (125 mL) white wine
  or cider
1 cup (250 mL) fresh seedless
  grapes
1/2 lb (250 g) pork sausages

Place the sauerkraut in a sieve and wash in hot water. Drain well.

Fry the onion in butter to a light brown. Add the sauerkraut and wine or cider. Cover and simmer over medium heat for 15 minutes. Fry the sausages, cut in 2-inch (5-cm) pieces. Drain from the fat and add to the sauerkraut. Simmer 5 minutes. Add the grapes. Simmer 1 minute. Serve with German mustard. Serves 4.

SAUSAGES AND APPLES

A Canadian special. Serve with toast, for a quick nourishing lunch.

1 lb (500 g) sausages
6 medium apples, unpeeled,
  sliced
1/4 tsp (1 mL) sage or savory

3 tbsp (50 mL) brown sugar
1/2 tsp (2 mL) cinnamon
1/4 tsp (1 mL) ground cloves

Fry the sausages in a large cast iron frying pan. When done remove from fat and set aside.

Slice the apples, add to all the fat remaining in the pan, sprinkle on the top the sage or savory, brown sugar, cinnamon and cloves.

Stir together over medium high heat for 2 to 3 minutes. Cover and cook 5 minutes, stirring once. Uncover, add the sausages, stir again and simmer another 5 minutes over low heat. Serves 4 to 6.

HAM

Ham is a big subject because there is a multitude of hams, all different in texture, shape and flavor. Large hams are costly, take a long time to simmer to the right tenderness, and require attention. However, ham steaks cut from the whole ham and quickly pan fried are a real treat, and the same steak can easily be turned into many interesting dishes when diced or chopped, or blended with different sauces and ingredients.

Another advantage is that pieces cut from the shoulder, i.e. the butt or cottage hams, can replace a more expensive steak from the whole leg of ham in any of the recipes. If you wish to simply and quickly pan fry a ham steak, you will find that it gives better results than from the ready-to-serve type. All ham steaks are pan broiled over medium heat: about 2 to 3 minutes on each side for a steak about 1/4-inch (0.5-cm) thick; a 1/2-inch (1.5-cm) slice will need 4 minutes on each side; 1-inch (2.5-cm) thick, 8 to 9 minutes. Try a ham loaf for a change from the usual, a ham en croûte for a buffet meal, a ham steak bigarade for sophistication.

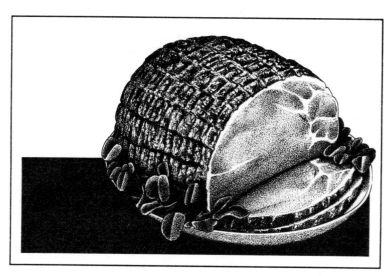

KITCHENER BAKED HAM

This makes a perfect buffet or cold supper **pièce de résistance**.

**10-15 lb (5 to 7 kg)
tenderized ham
1/2 cup (125 mL) brown
sugar
2 tsp (10 mL) dry mustard**

**2 tbsp (30 mL) rye or all
purpose flour
2 tbsp (30 mL) malt vinegar
whole cloves
1 pt (500 mL) light beer or
porter (dark brown beer)**

Bake the ham in a 300°F (150°C) oven for 4 hours, uncovered. Remove from dripping pan, drain the fat accumulated in the pan. Remove the skin from the ham and put back in the dripping pan. Mix the brown sugar, dry mustard, flour and vinegar into a paste. Score the ham in large diamonds, dot the middle of each diamond with a whole clove. Spread the paste over the top of the ham. Return to the oven for 40 minutes with the beer, then with the drippings in the bottom of the pan. Bake the last 15 minutes in a 400°F (200°C) oven. Serve hot or cold. Serves 15-20.

BIGARADE

Simple ingredients turn this ham steak into a distinguished dish. Served with parsleyed rice and corn niblets, it makes a pleasant family dinner.

**1 ham steak, 3/4-inch
(1.5 cm) thick
Kitchen Bouquet
1 tbsp (15 mL) salad oil
1 cup (250 mL) orange juice**

**1 tbsp (15 mL) butter
1/3 cup (80 mL) orange
marmalade
1/4 tsp (1 mL) ginger
1 tbsp (15 mL) cornstarch**

Trim any excess fat from the ham (I like to use a precooked or ready-to-serve type for this dish). Score fat along the edges. Brush all over with Kitchen Bouquet.

Heat the salad oil and brown ham steak on both sides, over medium heat. Remove to a platter and keep warm.

To the fat in the pan, add the orange juice, butter, marmalade, ginger and cornstarch. Cook, stirring all the time, until the sauce thickens, about 5 minutes. Put the ham in the sauce, cover and simmer over medium-low heat 10 minutes longer. To serve, cut into 1/2-inch (1.5 cm) slices across the grain. serves 6.

CHICKEN, CHICKEN

MAMAN'S CREAMY CHICKEN POT

In my family, this delicious creamed chicken was served the first Monday of every month. I still don't know why it was, but I do remember how eagerly we waited for that day. It was served with a large basket of hot biscuits and a salad of cabbage and apples.

1 boiling chicken*	1 parsley sprig
1 small onion	1/4 tsp (1 mL) mace
2 cloves	salt and pepper to taste
1 bay leaf	3 tbsp (50 mL) butter
3 cups (750 mL) milk (not homogenized)	3 tbsp (50 mL) all purpose flour
1 celery stalk and leaves, diced	

Stick the cloves in the onion and place inside the chicken. Tie the legs loosely. Place in a deep casserole and put the bay leaf on top. Add the milk, celery, parsley, mace, salt and pepper. Cover and bake at 275°F (135°C) for 2 to 3 hours, depending on the chicken.

When the bird is tender, remove from the dish and cut into pieces. Make a ball of the soft butter and flour, add to the hot milk and stir well until creamy. Taste for seasoning and pour over chicken. Serves 6-8.

*Any type of chicken can be used. Try it sometime with a small 6-to-8 lb (3-to-4 kg) turkey. Only the baking time will vary. If you prefer, cut the chicken before cooking and place the onion in the milk.

COLD BARBECUE

Cook this early in the morning and keep it at room temperature to serve at night. Hot rolls on the side are good for dipping into the tasty devilled sauce.

3 lb (1.5 kg) broiler, cut up
  or 3 lb (1.5 kg) chicken legs
4 tbsp (60 mL) salad
  oil or shortening
1 large onion, sliced
3 tbsp (50 mL) each brown
  sugar and cider vinegar
1/4 cup (60 mL) bottled
  lemon juice
1 cup (250 mL) tomato
  catsup

3 tbsp (50 mL) Worcestershire
  sauce
1 tbsp (15 mL) prepared
  mustard
1 1/4 cups (125 mL) water
1/2 cup diced celery
1/2 tsp (2 mL) each salt and
  oregano
1/4 tsp (1 mL) pepper

In a large frying pan, brown the chicken in the salad oil or shortening. As pieces are done, place them in a 3-quart (3 L) casserole. Add the remaining ingredients to the fat in pan, bring to a boil and pour over chicken. Cover and bake 1 hour in a 350°F (180°C) oven, then let cool. Uncover and let stand until needed. Serves 4 or 5.

GIANNINO LIME BROILED CHICKEN

A superb recipe from a justly famous restaurant in Milan, Italy, where the dark brown marble floor and huge cooking fireplace of azure tile make a perfect setting for the golden chicken. Serve this party dish hot or cold with a big bowl of plain watercress.

3 broiler-fryers, 2 1/2 to 3 lb (1 to 1.5 kg) each
3 tsp (15 mL) monosodium glutamate
1/2 cup (125 mL) bottled or fresh lime juice
1/2 cup (125 mL) olive oil or salad oil

grated peel of 2 limes
2 tbsp (30 mL) grated onion
1 tbsp (15 mL) tarragon
1 tsp (5 mL) salt
1/4 tsp (1 mL) hot pepper sauce

Preheat broiler. Cut each chicken into quarters and sprinkle with msg., salt and pepper to taste. Place skin side up on a broiler-rack, 6 inches (15 cm) from source of heat.

Whisk remaining ingredients together and brush onto each piece of chicken. Cook until tender, up to 1 hour, turning every 15 minutes and basting each time with the sauce.

If you have time, you can marinate the chicken pieces in the sauce overnight and turn them without basting when broiling. Serves 8 to 10.

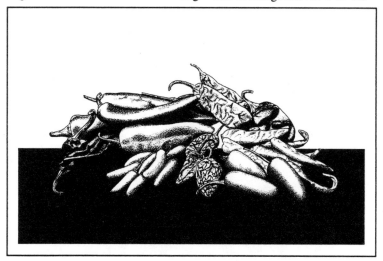

THREE KINDS OF CHOPS

BAKED PORK CHOPS

Tender, moist loin or rib pork chops baked in a sauce. Reheat or freeze. Will keep two months in freezer.

2 tbsp (30 mL) butter or olive oil
6 loin or rib pork chops, 3/4-inch (2-cm) thick
1 tsp (5 mL) sugar
salt and pepper
1 onion, chopped fine
1 small green pepper, diced

1 cup (250 mL) fresh mushrooms, sliced
1 8-oz (213 mL) can tomato sauce
1/4 tsp (1 mL) thyme
1 crumbled bay leaf
pinch of mace

Preheat oven to 350°F (180°C). In an iron frying pan, melt the butter or heat the olive oil. Rub one side of each chop with a bit of the teaspoon of sugar. Brown this side first. Brown the chops in the hot fat over high heat.

Arrange the chops, as they are browned, in a shallow 10 x 6 x 2-inch (25 x 15 x 5-cm) casserole dish. Salt and pepper to taste. To the fat remaining in the pan, add the onion and green pepper, stir 3 to 4 minutes over medium heat. Add the rest of the ingredients. Taste for seasoning. Bring to a boil and pour over the chops.

Cover the dish with a foil and bake one hour in the preheated oven. Serve with rice or fine noodles. Serves 6.

ITALIAN LAMB CHOPS

A specialty of Sienna.

6 loin or rib lamb chops
1 tbsp (15 mL) salad oil
1/2 tsp (2 mL) salt
1/2 tsp (2 mL) pepper
1/2 tsp (2 mL) basil or
  oregano

1 garlic clove, crushed
juice of 1 lemon
1/2 tsp (2 mL) French or
  German mustard

Remove excess fat from the chops. Mix the salad oil, salt, pepper, basil or oregano, and garlic and roll the chops in the mixture. Let them marinate in the liquid for 2 hours at room temperature.

Broil or pan fry, with or without fat. When ready to serve, set the chops on a hot platter and pour over the lemon juice mixed with the mustard.

FRENCH VEAL CHOPS

6 veal chops
2 tbsp (30 mL) veal
  kidney fat or
  1 tbsp (15 mL) butter

and 1 tbsp (15 mL)
  salad oil
salt and pepper to taste

Remove the bones from the chops and the hard skin around the meat. The chops can then be cooked as is, or may be flattened with a meat mallet for scalloped veal chops.

Melt the fat or heat the butter and salad oil in a frying pan. Add the chops and cook, uncovered, over medium heat for 15 to 20 minutes, turning once only.

Salt and pepper to taste and, if you wish to make a gravy, remove the chops from the pan before you start.

A STEW

My Finnish friend, Marta, who taught me how to make this so easy but so good meat stew, sometimes cooks it overnight on top of the stove over very low heat. Whichever way it's cooked, the result is superb. Serve with baked potatoes and pickled beet salad.

1 lb (500 g) shoulder pork,
  in one piece
1/2 lb (250 g) lean stewing
  beef
1 lb (500 g) shoulder lamb,
  in one piece
1 large onion, quartered

1 tsp (5 mL) salt
1 tsp (5 mL) black pepper,
  freshly ground
1 lemon slice, unpeeled
1 dried ginger root
hot water

Place all the ingredients in a Dutch oven or enamelled cast iron pan, using just enough hot water to cover them. Cover and bake at 325°F (165°C) for 4 to 5 hours, or over very low heat on top of the stove, until the meat is tender. The secret of this delicious boiled meat is to cook it so slowly that it never boils. The bouillon makes a delicious soup, or you can refrigerate it to use as stock. Baked potatoes will take 2 hours at 325°F (165°C). Serves 6.

A FEW CASSEROLES

LAMB AND BARLEY CASSEROLE

Barley is a natural convenience food with texture and flavor. Combined with lamb, flavored with orange and rosemary, it makes a true gourmet party dish, yet costs little and is quickly prepared.

**2-3 lb (1 to 1.5 kg)
  lamb shoulder
2 tbsp (30 mL) butter or
  salad oil
2 onions, chopped
1 cup (250 mL) pearl barley
2 unpeeled oranges, thinly
  sliced**

**1/4 tsp (1 mL) rosemary
juice of 1/2 a lemon
3 cups (750 mL) canned
  consommé, diluted or
  3 cups (750 mL) water
salt and pepper to taste**

Cut the lamb into individual pieces (2-3 cups [500 to 750 mL] of diced leftover lamb can replace the fresh). Brown it with the onion in butter or salad oil. Place in a casserole and add the rest of the ingredients. Cover and cook at 300°F (150°C) for 1 1/2 hours. Remove from oven, let stand 20 minutes before serving. Serves 6.

VEAL CASSEROLE

A casserole, flavored with tarragon and made creamy with a layer of shredded Swiss cheese. A truly great dish.

**4 tbsp (60 mL) butter
6 veal escalopes
salt and pepper
1/4 tsp (1 mL) tarragon
1 large mild onion, thinly
  sliced
1 cup (250 mL) shredded
  Swiss cheese**

**1/2 cup (125 mL) cracker
  crumbs
1/2 cup (125 mL) white wine
  or port wine
1/2 cup (125 mL) canned
  beef consommé, undiluted**

Melt 2 tablespoons (30 mL) of the butter in a large frying pan. Brown meat on both sides, over high heat. Place in a shallow baking dish, one next to the other. Salt and pepper lightly and sprinkle with the tarragon.

Cover each escalope first with a slice of onion, then cover the onion with grated cheese and top the cheese with crackers crumbs. Put a small dot of butter on top of each (use the remaining 2 tablespoons [30 mL] of butter). Pour half the mixed wine and consommé into the dish, letting liquid spread around the meat. Cover. Bake 45 minutes in a preheated 350°F (180°C) oven. Pour the rest of wine consommé mixture on top. Serves 4.

HAM ROSALIA

An elegant way to use a cup (250 mL) of leftover ham. Replace the leftover ham with cold roast pork.

2 tbsp (30 mL) butter
1/2 cup (125 mL) uncooked rice
1 onion, thinly sliced
1 green pepper, finely diced
1 cup (250 mL) water
1 tsp (5 mL) salt
1/4 tsp (1 mL) pepper
2 tbsp (30 mL) butter

2 tbsp (30 mL) flour
2 cups (500 mL) milk
2 egg yolks, well beaten
1 cup (250 mL) minced cooked ham
1/4 cup (60 mL) grated cheese (optional)
2 egg whites

Place the first 2 tablespoons (30 mL) of butter in a saucepan. When melted, add the rice, onion and green pepper. Stir over medium heat until the onion is soft and the rice well buttered. Add the water, salt and pepper. Bring to the boil. Cover and simmer 15 minutes.

In the meantime, make a white sauce with the 2 remaining tablespoons (30 mL) butter, the flour and the milk. When smooth and creamy, remove from heat. Mix the egg yolks with a few spoonfuls of the hot sauce. Add to the sauce, stir thoroughly, add the ham and the grated cheese. Season to taste. Beat the egg whites until stiff. Fold into the sauce.

Butter a casserole, place a layer of the cooked rice in the bottom, cover with a layer of the ham sauce. Repeat until all the ingredients have been used. Sprinkle a little cheese on top. Bake in a 375 °F (190°C) oven for 30 minutes or until well browned on top. Serves 4 to 6.

Fish

FISH

Fish, **at no time**, should be overcooked because it then becomes tough and dry. A good rule to apply is to cook any fish 10 minutes per inch (2.5 cm) of thickness (measure at its thickest part).

A half pound (225 g) of dressed or cleaned fish or frozen or fresh fillets will serve one.

A third of a pound (150 g) of fish steaks will serve one.

General Information

- In any recipe you can substitute other fish for the ones that are specified.
- Any large fish may be baked, with or without stuffing, or steamed.
- Any fish steak may be broiled, baked, or poached.
- Any fillet may be sautéed, poached, panfried, or baked in a sauce.
- Citrus fruit such as lemon, lime, grapefruit and orange make marvellous endings for fish dinners.

The Chinese method of broiling fish

Water is the secret of this method. High heat is used as the fish is protected by the humidity of the water.

- Place the fillets on an oiled rack set in a shallow boiling pan.
- Sprinkle (do not roll) the fillets generously with fine breadcrumbs and dot with butter.
- Pour 1/4 inch (1 cm) of hot water in the pan.
- Preheat broiler to 550°F (285°C) or for 15 minutes. This is important.
- Set the broiler pan 3 to 4 inches (7.5 to 10 cm) from the source of heat.
- Broil **exactly** 5 minutes, unless you are broiling very thin fillets which may take only 3 minutes.

Pan fried frozen fillets

Pan frying frozen fillets has several disadvantages. They are more difficult to cook this way; the pan is usually hard to clean; and if the moisture is not well taken care of, the fat will spatter.

This is the way to proceed:
- Completely thaw the fish in the refrigerator. Open box and wrap each fillet in a piece of absorbent paper. Refrigerate 1 hour.
- Sprinkle both sides of fillets with salt, pepper and paprika.
- Roll in fine dry breadcrumbs or fine cracker crumbs or flour. Let the fish stand for 10 minutes, the coating will dry the top of the fish.

- Fry fish in 1/8 inch (0.5 cm) of just hot salad oil, or half oil and half butter. Fry over medium low heat, turning the fish **only once**. Use a spatula to turn the fish.

- The cooking takes 10 minutes per inch (2.5 cm) of thickness. Measure at the thickest part of the fish before cooking. If only 1/2-inch (1.2-cm) thick, 5 minutes are required, etc.

- Turn the fillets when 2 minutes of the cooking time are left.

- **Warning**: If a second batch of fish has to be cooked, wipe the hot pan clean with absorbent paper and add fresh fat; otherwise the second batch will have burnt spots and the fine taste of the fish will be lost.

COD FILLETS GRAPEFRUIT

Fillets or steaks can be used, fresh or frozen. This is unusual and most pleasant.

6 cod fillets or steaks
seasoned flour
2 tbsp (30 mL) butter
3 tbsp (50 mL) salad oil

1/4 cup (60 mL) cream
1 large grapefruit
2 hard cooked eggs
chopped parsley

Roll the fillets or steaks in the seasoned flour. Heat the butter and salad oil in a large cast iron frying pan. Brown the fillets over medium heat, about 10 to 12 minutes, turning only once.

In a small saucepan heat 1 tablespoon (15 mL) butter, add the cream and the juice of 1/2 the grapefruit. Chop the eggs and add. Heat together, but do not boil. Salt and pepper to taste. Set the fish on a hot platter and pour the sauce over. Sprinkle with parsley.

Cut the other half of the grapefruit in two and slice thinly. Place around the fish. Serves 6.

BROWN BUTTER HALIBUT

A "take-off" from the classic Eggs au Beurre Noir. Served with buttered long grain rice and green peas flavored with fresh mint, it is a meal to please the most demanding.

4 halibut steaks
1/2 cup (125 mL) milk
1/2 tsp (2 mL) salt
1/4 tsp (1 mL) freshly
  ground pepper

grated rind of 1/2 a lemon
1/4 cup (60 mL) flour
1 tbsp (15 mL) butter
2 tbsp (30 mL) salad oil

Brown butter

1 tbsp (15 mL) cider
vinegar
2 to 3 tbsp (30 to 50 mL)
butter

1 tbsp (15 mL) parsley,
finely minced

Mix the milk with the salt, pepper and grated lemon rind. Measure the flour onto a meat plate. Roll each halibut steak in the seasoned milk, then roll in the flour. Heat the 1 tablespoon (15 mL) butter with the salad oil in a frying pan. When hot, put in the halibut steak and fry over medium heat 4 minutes per side, turning only once. Set on a hot platter.

To make the brown butter: add the vinegar first to the fat left in the frying pan; set over high heat; add the butter; stir quickly without a stop until the butter has a nutty brown color; pour over the halibut and serve.

To make Halibut Amandine, proceed in the same way, adding 1/4 cup (60 mL) of blanched almonds, cut into long slivers, at the same time the butter is added. The almonds will brown as fast as the butter. Serves 4.

Sole Bercy →

WREXHAN FINNAN SPAGHETTI

English farmhouse native cooking, the recipe was given to me by Mrs. Cowking, who had inherited it from her grandmother and mother. That was many years ago, in 1945 to be exact. I still enjoy making it.

1 lb (500 g) Finnan Haddie	3 tbsp (50 mL) flour
1/4 tsp (1 mL) savory	2 cups (500 mL) milk
8 ounces (232 g) spaghetti or	salt, pepper to taste
elbow macaroni	1/2 to 3/4 cup (125 to 190 mL)
4 slices bacon	grated cheese
1 large onion, thinly sliced	1/8 tsp (0.5 mL) nutmeg
3 tbsp (50 mL) butter	1 cup (250 mL) diced bread

Place the fish in a sauce pan with 2 cups boiling water and the savory. Cover and simmer over low heat for 10 minutes. Remove to a plate, cool and flake.

Boil the spaghetti or elbow macaroni according to directions given on the package. Drain and place in a bowl. Dice and fry the bacon, add the onion and fry until light brown. Add to the spaghetti with the flaked fish.

Make a white sauce with the butter, flour and milk. When smooth and creamy, salt and pepper to taste, remove from heat, and add the cheese and nutmeg. Place the fish mixture in a casserole dish. Pour the cheese sauce over all. Top with the diced bread that can be rolled, to taste, in a few tablespoons of bacon fat or melted butter. Bake in a 350°F (180°C) oven for 25 to 30 minutes. Serve hot. Serves 6.

← *Poached Salmon à la française*

POACHED SALMON À LA FRANÇAISE

The French use salmon steak for this colorful and tasty dish. It is then as easy to make for 2 as for 10. It is served with the classic **sauce verte**.

4 - 6 salmon steaks
1 tbsp (15 mL) salad oil
juice of 1 lemon
peel of 1/2 lemon, grated

6 peppercorns, crushed with
  back of spoon
1 tbsp (15 mL) salt
1 small onion, quartered
3 - 6 sprigs parsley

Spread the oil in a frying pan (I like to use the teflon coated type), or in a flat baking dish. Place the salmon slices next to one another, but not overlapping. Add the lemon juice and peel, peppercorns, salt, onion and enough hot water to just cover the fish. Cover and poach on top of the stove (if in frying pan) over low heat for 10 - 20 minutes; or in a 325°F (165°C) oven (in baking dish) for the same length of time, or until the salmon flakes. Allow the fish to cool in the liquid. Drain well and remove the skin. Arrange on a serving platter, then completely cover the fish with the following sauce. Serve with a cucumber salad. Serves 4 - 6.

SAUCE VERTE

If you have a blender, this sauce will be ready in minutes. If not, the ingredients will have to be chopped very finely.

1/2 cup (125 mL) green onion
  tops or chives
1/2 cup (125 mL) green
  pepper
1/4 cup (60 mL) parsley

1/2 cup (125 mL) spinach,
  uncooked
2 tbsp (30 mL) lemon juice
1 cup (250 mL) mayonnaise

Chop the vegetables coarsley and place in blender with lemon juice. Cover and blend until it turns into a sort of mush with small bits of this and that in it. Add to the mayonnaise and blend.

Without the blender, chop the ingrediens very finely and blend into the mayonnaise, crushing them to give as much color as possible to the sauce. Makes 1 1/2 cups (375 mL).

SOLE BERCY

This one tops my list of favorites for its simplicity. It is the different possible combinations of ingredients that give each variation of this dish a special finish.

2 French shallots or 4 green onions
1/4 cup (60 mL) chopped fresh parsley or 1 tbsp (15 mL) dried parsley
1/4 cup (60 mL) white wine
1/4 cup (60 mL) fish fumet or clam juice

1 - 2 lb (500 g to 1 kg) fillets of sole
juice of 1/2 a lemon
3 tbsp (50 mL) butter, salted or unsalted
finely chopped parsley

Sprinkle the shallots or onions and the parsley over the bottom of a generously buttered, shallow baking dish, then add wine and fumet or clam juice. Lightly salt and pepper both sides of the fillets, and set over ingredients in baking dish (they can be placed side by side, slightly overlapping, or folded in three). Sprinkle with lemon juice and dot with butter.

Cook uncovered in a 350°F (180°C) oven 20 minutes, basting twice with pan liquid, then broil a few seconds to brown here and there. This is good surrounded by small boiled potatoes. Garnish all with parsley and serve immediately. Serves 6.

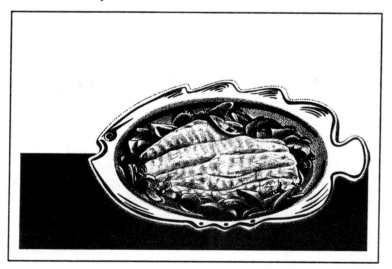

TROUT MEUNIÈRE

Another French specialty, this one is very popular with men as lunch time dish. Though extra delightful with fresh trout, it is also very good prepared with frozen speckled trout (all kinds are good, of course, but not so readily available).

2 lb (1 kg) fresh or frozen
  trout
4 tbsp (60 mL) flour
1/2 tsp (2 mL) salt
1/4 tsp (1 mL) pepper
1/8 tsp (0.5) thyme

1/2 tsp (2 mL) paprika
1 tbsp (15 mL) salad oil
4 tbsp (60 mL) butter
juice of 1/2 lemon
1 tbsp (15 mL) finely
  chopped parsley

Thaw the frozen trout or wash the fresh type thoroughly. Using scissors, trim fins close to the skin, accentuating the tail by cutting it into a V-shape to make two distinct points. Roll fish in a mixture of flour and seasonings.

Heat oil and 2 tbsp (30 mL) of the butter in a heavy frying pan, and cook fish over medium heat about 6 minutes per side, turning once only, until golden brown. Place on a hot serving dish and keep warm. Wipe frying pan with paper towels, then add remaining butter and cook over medium heat until nutty brown. Add lemon juice, salt and pepper to taste. Pour over fish while still foaming, sprinkle parsley on top, and serve immediately. Serves 4.

ENGLISH FISH SALAD

This salad is so good that whenever I cook fish I usually do more than I need so I can make it. Any poached, fried or steamed fish will do, but fried cod, haddock and halibut are the best.

1/2 lb (250 g) cooked fish
3 - 4 cooked potatoes, thinly
  sliced
1 medium onion, thinly sliced
2 tomatoes, peeled and sliced
2 tbsp (30 mL) salad oil

1 tbsp (15 mL) cider or wine
  vinegar
1 tbsp (15 mL) strong
  prepared mustard
1/2 tsp (2 mL) salt
1/4 tsp (1 mL) each pepper
  and turmeric

Break fish into pieces, removing any skin. In a salad bowl make alternate layers of fish, potatoes, onion and tomatoes. Beat remaining ingredients with a rotatry beater and pour over salad. If you wish, surround with a border of finely chopped parsley or chives. Cover and refrigerate 3 - 5 hours before serving. Serves 2-3.

CHINESE SWEET AND SOUR TUNA

This is a quick delight for those who like Chinese Sweet and Sour food. Albacore or other types can be used, the flavor will be just as good, but the appearance of the dish is better with Albacore tuna.

6 slices canned pineapple
2 tbsp (30 mL) butter
2/3 cup (160 mL) of the
  pineapple syrup or 2/3 cup
  (160 mL) pineapple juice
2 green peppers
2 tbsp (30 mL) cornstarch
2 tsp (10 mL) soy sauce

2 tbsp (30 mL) cider vinegar
2 tbsp (30 mL) sugar
1 cup (250 mL) chicken
  bouillon or consommé
2 cans tuna
1/2 tsp (2 mL) salt
1/4 tsp (1 mL) pepper

Drain pineapple and cut each slice into sixths. Sauté in the butter over high heat for about 5 minutes. Add 1/3 cup (80 mL) of the pineapple juice (the juice is better than the syrup because it has more piquancy) and the green pepper.

Mix the cornstarch with the remaining 1/3 cup (80 mL) of pineapple juice. Add to pineapple mixture with the soy sauce, vinegar, sugar and bouillon or consommé. Cook over medium heat, stirring constantly, until thick and creamy. Add the tuna, undrained, salt and pepper. Heat thoroughly. Serve with boiled rice. Serves 6.

SCALLOPED SARDINES

The Scandinavian countries have long known the pleasure of eating golden scalloped potatoes with sardines. It is a gourmet dish at low cost.

3 - 4 medium potatoes,
  peeled
2 medium onions, thinly
  sliced
2 cans sardines, well-drained
3 eggs

1/2 tsp (2 mL) turmeric
pinch of nutmeg
1 1/2 cups (375 mL) milk
4 tbsp (60 mL) butter,
  melted

Grease a 1 1/2 quart (1.8 L) casserole with butter. Cover bottom with a layer of thinly sliced, raw potatoes; brush with a bit of melted butter. Place a layer of onions on top, then a layer of sardines. Salt and pepper lightly.

Repeat layers, but change the order so that the next layer will be onion, the next sardines and the top layer potatoes. Beat the eggs with the turmeric and nutmeg. Add milk and melted butter, salt and pepper to taste. Pour over potatoes and bake at 350°F (180°C) for 50 - 60 minutes, or until the potatoes are tender and golden. Serves 4 - 6.

BUTTERFLY SHRIMP

Through the years, I have been asked for this recipe more often than any other. Not only shrimp but squares of halibut or pieces of lobster can be prepared in this way. Of course, they will not be "butterfly" but the succulent taste will be the same.

1 lb (500 g) raw shrimp,
  shelled
1 tbsp (15 mL) soy sauce
1 tsp (5 mL) sherry
1/2 tsp (2 mL) salt
1/4 tsp (1 mL) monosodium
  glutamate

thick slice fresh ginger,
  peeled and grated
2 eggs, beaten
1 1/2 tbsp (22 mL)
  cornstarch
1 1/2 tbsp (22 mL) flour
corn or peanut oil for frying

Cut shelled shrimp halfway through on inner curve and spread out to form a butterfly. The cutting is done with scissors or a sharp knife.

Mix together the soy sauce, sherry, salt, monosodium glutamate and grated ginger. Roll shrimp in this mixture and marinate for 15 minutes to an hour. Remove from mixture and dry thoroughly with absorbent paper. Mix the eggs, cornstarch and flour and dip each shrimp in this mixture until well coated. Fry the shrimp in 2 inches (5 cm) of hot oil until they are golden, and serve while hot. Serves 4.

LOBSTER CARDINAL

Using fresh, frozen or even canned lobster, this dish will be spectacular and delicious. Part of the work is done early in the morning; the last touches take only a few minutes to do in your chafing dish.

2 tbsp (30 mL) flour
3/4 cup (190 mL) light cream
1 tsp (5 mL) curry powder
1/2 tsp (2 mL) turmeric
salt and pepper to taste
4 tbsp (60 mL) brandy or
  whisky
2/3 cup (160 mL) tomato
  sauce

1/4 tsp (1 mL) tarragon
1/2 tsp (2 mL) sugar
3 tbsp (50 mL) butter
1 - 1 1/2 lb (500 - 700 g)
  lobster meat
1 cup (250 mL) long grain
  rice

In the morning, blend the flour with the cream until smooth, then cook over low heat, stirring all the time, until creamy. Add the curry powder, turmeric, salt and pepper.

Beat with a whisk or a hand beater until the sauce is well blended. Pour into an attractive container. Cover with a piece of waxed paper, with the paper touching the sauce to prevent a crust forming.

On a tray, place the container of cream sauce and, in small bowls, the brandy or whisky, and the tomato sauce stirred with the tarragon and sugar. Add a wooden spoon to cook with, and a medium-sized serving spoon. Get your chafing dish (or any other utensil you wish to cook with) ready to be taken out. Keep the butter and lobster refrigerated until you are ready to start cooking.

To make the rice ahead of time: boil it according to the package directions. Drain, then rinse under running cold water. Pour into a baking dish that has a cover. Place dots of butter on top of the rice. Salt and pepper lightly and cover. About 5 minutes before serving, place the dish over low heat, covered. After 5 minutes, stir with a fork. It will be hot and ready to serve.

To finish the Lobster Cardinal, melt the butter in a chafing dish over a good flame, or in an electric frying pan at 350°F (180°C). Add the lobster, and stir for a few minutes to warm it up. Pour the brandy or whisky on top and warm up for 2 - 4 seconds. Set a match to it and blaze. Add the cooked cream sauce and the tomato sauce mixture. Stir gently until the whole is well mixed and hot.

This is very nice served **à la Chinoise** in small individual bowls. The rice can be served in one large bowl, or in a separate bowl for each guest. Serves 4.

SAUTÉED SCALLOP REMOULADE

The Remoulade sauce, similar to but more delicate than tartar, is the best choice with sautéed or pan-fried scallops, be they breaded or plain.

1 lb (500 g) scallops
1 tsp (5 mL) salt
1/4 tsp (1 mL) pepper
2 eggs
2 tbsp (30 mL) milk

1 cup (250 mL) fine bread or
    cracker crumbs
salad oil
Remoulade Sauce (see below)

If frozen, thaw and dry the scallops, then sprinkle with the salt and pepper. Dip each into eggs beaten with milk, then roll in crumbs and let dry 15 - 20 minutes, uncovered, on a platter. Heat 1/4 inch (0.7 cm) of salad oil in a cast iron frying pan, but don't let it smoke. Fry scallops over moderate heat, 3 minutes per side, or until golden brown. Set on a warm platter and serve the following sauce separately. Serves 6.

Remoulade Sauce: Combine 1 cup (250 mL) of mayonnaise, 2 teaspoons (10 mL) of prepared French mustard, 2 small minced gherkins, 1 tablespoon (15 mL) each of capers and chopped parsley, 1/2 teaspoon (2 mL) of dried tarragon, 1 small, finely chopped onion, salt and pepper to taste. Yield: 1 1/4 cups (315 mL).

CRAB QUICHE

I learned to make this while spending a few days with a fisherman's family in Covey Cove, N.S. This is my variation of his wife's lobster pie.

pie crust of your choice, thinly rolled
1 cup (250 mL) mushrooms, sliced
2 tbsp (30 mL) brandy or lemon juice
1 cup (250 mL) canned crab

1/4 lb (113 g) Swiss or mild Cheddar cheese, grated
3 eggs
1 tbsp (15 mL) all purpose flour
1/8 tsp (0.5 mL) nutmeg
1/2 tsp (2 mL) salt
1 cup (250 mL) cream

Line 8 2-inch (5-cm) aluminum tart pans with the thinly rolled pastry. Preheat oven to 375°F (190°C). Combine and stir the mushrooms with the brandy or lemon juice, then shred the crab, removing any hard parts. Fill each tart with alternate layers of sliced mushrooms, crab and grated cheese. Beat together the eggs, flour, nutmeg, salt and cream, then pour equally over each tart. Place in a baking pan and bake for 20 - 30 minutes, or until the custard is set and the top golden brown. Serves 8.

If you are preparing this in advance, cool thoroughly and wrap each tart individually in a square of foil. Refrigerate or freeze. To reheat, unwrap and place in a 375°F (190°C) oven for 10 - 15 minutes.

Vegetables

VEGETABLES

It is a fact that, artfully cooked and seasoned, vegetables can make satis-fying dinners. The one important factor is that most vegetables should be cooked as briefly as possible to retain the most flavor, texteure, vita-mins and minerals and as well to be at their most attractive in appear-ance. Much has been said about the importance of saving the liquid in which vegetables are cooked; but what is much more important is to use as little liquid as possible, even, when possible, to cook the vegeta-bles in butter or salad oil without water or simply steam them.

NEW IDEAS WITH VEGETABLES

Use these or make variations to suit your fancy.

BEETS. Cook small unpeeled beets until tender, rub off skins, cut into wedges, and serve hot or cold with sour cream blended to taste with horseradish and lemon juice or orange rind.

BROCCOLI. Add coarsely chopped brocoli stems and small pieces of green tops to partly cooked elbow macaroni in cheese sauce. Pour into a casserole, top with grated cheese and crumbled saltines, dot with butter, and bake.

CARROTS. Scrape tiny carrots and cut into lengthwise quarters. Steam covered tightly in a little salted water until just tender. Drain well. Sauté in butter until lightly browned and top with melted currant jelly to taste.

CAULIFLOWER. In a small frying pan, sauté a little minced onion in butter, blend it into a thick cheese sauce with chopped cooked shrimp and seasonings. Pour over firmly cooked cauliflower flowerets. Garnish with chopped capers.

EGGPLANT. Peel and dice eggplant, salt well, and allow to stand for 1 hour. Drain. Sauté in butter with grated onion and turmeric, and cook covered, until just tender. Serve hot or chilled. Delectable.

GREEN BEANS. Snap ends off fresh firm green beans, and cook in a small amount of lightly salted water until just tender. Drain and arrange neatly in an ovenproof casserole. Add cream to taste, dot liberally with butter, sprinkle with pepper, and run under broiler until bubbling.

GREEN PEPPERS. Toast fork-speared peppers over an open flame until charred on all sides, rub off skins under running water. Slice thickly, and marinate in piquant vinaigrette dressing. Serve drained as antipasto or hors d'oeuvre.

PEAS. To any omelet, add 1 cup (250 mL) or more cooked peas, slivers of cooked ham, and a little grated green pepper. Cook, fold and serve.

RED RADISH. Carefully scoop out radishes with vegetable peeler, leaving firm shell. Sprinkle with salt, and stuff with blended cream, blue or Cheddar cheese. It is an act of patience but well worth it!

WATERCRESS. Snip crisp watercress finely with kitchen shears. Add slivered toasted almonds, and fold into baked potato that has been scraped from jacket and whipped with butter. Return to jacket.

ASPARAGUS and CAULIFLOWER. Fresh, frozen or canned. Cook or heat and sprinkle with browned buttered breadcrumbs.

ANY CANNED VEGETABLE. Boil the juice drained from any canned vegetable with a thick slice of onion chopped fine, a pinch of sugar and salt. When the juice is reduced by half, add the vegetables and cook quickly just to heat through.

CANNED ONIONS. Drain and mix onions with undiluted cream of celery soup plus 1/2 cup (125 mL) of cream and 1/4 teaspoon (1 mL) curry. Season to taste.

CANNED TOMATOES. Pour a 19-oz (540 mL) can of tomatoes into a baking dish. Top with 1 cup (250 mL) of diced bread, 1/2 teaspoon (2 mL) thyme, salt and pepper to taste, 1 tablespoon (15 mL) sugar, 1 tablespoon (15 mL) lemon juice and 4 tablespoons (60 mL) butter. Place for 30 minutes in a 400°F (200°C) oven.

HOW TO SERVE ASPARAGUS

Asparagus Amandine

Place cooked drained asparagus on hot platter. Sauté 1/4 cup (60mL) slivered blanched almonds in 3 tablespoons (50 mL) butter until they are a light brown color. Salt and pepper asparagus and pour the sautéed nuts on top.

Asparagus Hollandaise

Prepare 1 cup (250 mL) Hollandaise Sauce for 1 to 2 pounds (500 g to 1 kg) cooked asparagus. Serve separately. OR make 1 cup (250 mL) light white sauce: 1 tablespoon (15 mL) butter, 1 tablespoon (15 mL) flour, 1 cup (250 mL) milk. Beat in an egg yolk mixed with the juice of 1/2 to 1 lemon. This is mock Hollandaise.

Creamed Asparagus

Place the cooked asparagus, left whole or diced, in a vegetable dish. Salt and pepper lightly, make a well seasoned medium white sauce, flavor to taste with lemon juice or mild grated cheese or 1 or 2 tablespoons (15 or 30 mL) of mayonnaise, then pour over the asparagus. Contrary to other vegetables, never mix asparagus with the sauce.

Asparagus Italian

Place cooked asparagus on a heatproof dish, pour melted butter on top, about 2 tablespoons (30 mL) per pound (500 g). Sprinkle grated Parmesan on the stalks but not on the heads. Broil under direct heat for 1 1/2 to 2 minutes and serve.

Asparagus à l'Espagnole

Place the hot cooked asparagus in a heap in the middle of a warm platter. Surround with poached eggs. Pour well flavored, thick tomato sauce over the eggs. Serve as a main course.

Asparagus à la Française

Place the cooked asparagus on a hot service plater. Fan the stalk ends, but keep the heads together. Pour the following sauce on top and serve.

Have all the ingredients at room temperature. Whip 2/3 cup (160 mL) cream. Add 1/4 teaspoon (1 mL) nutmeg, 3 tablespoons (50 mL) melted butter and 1/3 cup (80 mL) grated Swiss cheese. Pile this cloudy light sauce in the middle of the asparagus and serve.

Asparagus Hungarian Style

Place cooked asparagus in a shallow baking dish. Mix together 1 cup (250 mL) sour cream, 2 tablespoons (30 mL) lemon juice, salt, pepper to taste and warm slightly, but do not boil. Pour over the asparagus. Brown in 2 tablespoons (30 mL) butter 1/2 cup (125 mL) fresh dry crumbs, broken into small pieces. When light brown, pour over the cream sauce. Enough for one to two pounds (500 g to 1 kg) of asparagus.

Asparagus Dutch Style

Place individual portions of hot cooked asparagus on a hot plate. Quarter 1 hard cooked egg, place attractively around the asparagus, sprinkle with salt, pepper and a dash of nutmeg. Serve with a tureen of melted butter. Everyone mashes a portion of egg, sprinkles it over the asparagus and pours melted butter to taste on the whole. A very nice spring lunch served with milk cheese and toasted French bread.

Asparagus, Chinese Style

Cut cleaned, uncooked asparagus, with a sharp knife on a very long, slanting diagonal to the end of the green length of stalk up to the head.

For one pound (500 g) of asparagus, sprinkle the bottom of a large hot frying pan with 1/2 teaspoon (2 mL) salt, add 3 tablespoons (50 mL) salad oil, preferably peanut oil. When the oil is hot, add the prepared asparagus. Stir over high heat, constantly, until each piece is coated with oil. Add 1/4 cup (60 mL) chicken broth or water. Cover and cook 5 minutes. Shake frying pan occasionally, but without removing cover. Uncover. Serve quickly.

Asparagus American Style

Soften over low heat a 3-oz (85-g) package of chives or plain cream cheese with 1 tablespoon (15 mL) cream or milk. Stir until smooth and use as a sauce over or with cooked asparagus.

Hot Asparagus Salad

Beat together 2 small green onions, finely chopped, 1 teaspoon (5 mL) sugar, 1 tablespoon (15 mL) cider vinegar, 1 teaspoon (5 mL) capers, 1/4 teaspoon (1 mL) paprika, 1/2 teaspoon (2 mL) salt, 1/2 cup (125 mL) sour cream. Brown lightly in butter, 1/2 cup (125 mL) bread croutons. Add to dressing. Place hot cooked asparagus, cut in two, in a salad bowl, toss with sour cream dressing and serve.

Asparagus Salad, Grand Vatel

Combine the following ingredients in a bottle, 3/4 teaspoon (3 mL) salt, 1/4 teaspoon (1 mL) pepper, 1/4 teaspoon (1 mL) sugar, 1/4 cup (60 mL) fresh lime juice, 3/4 cup (190 mL) salad oil, 1 clove garlic peeled but left whole. Shake until well blended. This lime dressing will keep, refrigerated, for 3 to 4 weeks.

Hard cook and grate 4 eggs.

Cook one pound (500 g) asparagus, cut into 3-inch (7.5-cm) lengths. Drain and cool. Place in a bowl, add a few spoonfuls of lime dressing and toss lightly until well coated. Place in a salad bowl, completely cover with the grated eggs, and surround with a ring of watercress or shredded lettuce.

BEETS, CABBAGE,
CAULIFLOWER AND TURNIPS

There are more than one way of serving them as all countries of the world have used these vegetables for ever so long and created with them tasty and interesting dishes. They can be turned into soups, main dishes and appetizers as well as being a plain buttered hot vegetable. Above all, they should never be overcooked.

If you wish to get acquainted with their fine flavor, brilliant colors and crispness, try cooking them following my favorite pan cooking method.

In a heavy wide saucepan with a well fitting cover, melt and ever so slightly brown 1 1/2 tablespoons (22 mL) of butter for 4 heaping cups (1 L) of the vegetable measured after dicing, slicing, chopping, or grating the peeled raw beets or the peeled raw turnip or the cabbage.

Over the butter pour 1/2 inch (1.5 cm) boiling water. Add 1/2 teaspoon (2 mL) sugar and spread on top the prepared vegetable. Cover and boil 1 minute. Then reduce the heat to quite low and steam 10 to 25 minutes, according to the vegetable texture and the size of the pieces.

Shake the pan, without uncovering, 3 to 4 times during the cooking process. Serve as is as soon as ready. To taste, a sprinkling of salt can be added, but taste them without salt, you will be pleasantly surprised.

CONNOISSEUR FLAVORS

— After pan cooking the turnips try this. Place in a pan the grated rind and juice of 1 orange, 1 tablespoon (15 mL) whipping cream. Just bring to the boil (the orange juice will thicken the cream), and add the cooked turnip. Swirl together for a few seconds. Salt and pepper to taste and serve.

— If you wish, replace the orange juice and rind by 1/4 teaspoon (1 mL) basil and a sprinkling of nutmeg.

— After pan cooking the shredded cabbage, add to it 1 teaspoon (5 mL) curry powder, 1/4 teaspoon (1 mL) dill seed, salt and pepper to taste, and 1 tablespoon (15 mL) butter. Swirl together with a fork and serve.

— After pan cooking the beets, add 1 unpeeled apple grated, the juice of 1/2 lemon, 1 teaspoon (5 mL) sugar, a pinch of cloves and cinnamon, 1 teaspoon (5 mL) butter. Swirl together over low heat for 2 to 3 minutes and serve.

YOUNG BEETS IN SOUR CREAM

In a rush use well drained canned beets; of course fresh boiled young garden beets are the best.

2 bunches cooked new beets	**1/4 tsp (1 mL) nutmeg**
3 tbsp (50 mL) butter	**1 tbsp (15 mL) honey**
2 tbsp (30 mL) lemon juice	**minced onion to taste**
seasoned salt to taste	**1/2 to 3/4 cup (125 to 190 mL)**
fresh ground pepper to taste	**sour cream**

Peel and grate the cooked beets. Place in a saucepan, add the other ingredients. Stir over low heat until well blended and hot. Serves 6.

TYROLEAN CABBAGE

Serve with boiled ham and baked potatoes.

5 cups (1.2 L) shredded
  cabbage
4 tbsp (60 mL) bacon fat
1 onion, minced

3/4 tsp (3 mL) salt
1/8 tsp (0.5 mL) pepper
1 cup (250 mL) sour cream

Melt the bacon fat in a large frying pan, add the cabbage and the onion.
Cook over medium heat for 5 to 8 minutes, stirring often. Season. Place
in a buttered baking dish, pour the sour cream over, bake 25 minutes
in a 350°F (180°C) oven. Serves 6.

GOLDEN CAULIFLOWER

Cauliflower is the flower of the cabbage family and should be treated
as its position merits. When possible, steam the flowerets of cauliflower for perfection. This sauce over the cauliflower gets its regal color
from the turmeric.

1 cauliflower
1 tbsp (15 mL) cider vinegar
1 tsp (5 mL) sugar
1 cup (250 mL) boiling water
2 tbsp (30 mL) butter

3 tbsp (50 mL) lemon juice
1 tsp (5 mL) turmeric
2 tsp (10 mL) cornstarch
salt and pepper to taste

Break the cauliflower into small flowerets, chop the tenderest leaves and
grate the core. Place all in a saucepan, add the vinegar and sugar. (This
keeps the cauliflower white.) Add the boiling water. Stir. Cover and
boil 5 to 7 minutes. Drain, reserving the water. Place the cauliflower
in a hot serving dish. Mix the cornstarch with the lemon juice and add
to the reserved water with the rest of the ingredients. Stir over medium
heat until creamy and hot. Pour over the cauliflower and serve. Serves 4.

TURNIPS À LA FRANÇAISE

A pleasant winter supper.

2 cups (500 mL) mashed
   cooked turnip
1 egg
2 tbsp (30 mL) butter
1/8 tsp (0.5 mL) savory
salt and pepper to taste

3 tbsp (50 mL) flour
3 tbsp (50 mL) butter
1 cup (250 mL) milk
1/2 cup (125 mL) grated
   cheese

Pan cook and mash the turnip, add the egg, the 2 tablespoons (30 mL) of butter, the savory, salt and pepper to taste. Beat together until well blended. Place in a buttered baking dish in a mound.

Make a white sauce with the 3 tablespoons (50 mL) butter, flour and milk. Season to taste and pour over the turnip. Top the whole with the grated cheese. Bake 20 minutes in a 400°F (200°C) oven. Serve as a main dish with crisp buttered toast. Serves 4.

CARROTS

If to the culinary pleasures you add the fact that diet wise the carrot is an important vegetable, rich in carotene, with more Vitamin A than other vegetables, good for the skin and eyes, there is little excuse for the neglect we demonstrate towards this colorful root. I have two favorite spreads that can be made in two minutes, if you have a blender, or in 5 by hand, and they are versatile since they can be shaped into little balls to garnish your fruit salad or made a bit creamier for use as a dip. The first is my honey-carrot spread. I scrub 3 carrots with a stiff brush, then I pass them over a fine grater. I add 2 tablespoons (30 mL) orange juice, the grated rind of 1/2 an orange and 3 to 4 tablespoons (50 to 60 mL) cream cheese. Mash and blend, et voilà! To make it clearer I add a bit of sour or rich cream. In the blender, I put the orange juice and rind, the honey and the sliced carrots on top, I blend, then add the cream cheese by hand.

The second one is my carrot-nut spread. I use it as a sandwich spread; to garnish a consommé with a teaspoon (5 mL) in each plate; as a dip with sour cream added; or mixed with a cup (250 mL) of cottage cheese to serve with lettuce. For this spread, I scrape and grate finely 2 medium carrots, then I add 1 cup (250 mL) chopped walnuts or pecans, 1 tablespoon (15 mL) peanut oil, 1 tablespoon (15 mL) lemon juice, 2 sprigs fresh dill chopped or 1/4 cup (60 mL) chopped fresh parsley. Mash and blend in the bowl and use.

RUSSIAN BRAISED CARROTS

If you sometimes enjoy a vegetarian dish, try this one. In the summer, I like to sprinkle the top with a bit of chives and basil fresh from the garden. Very good in a vegetable plate with a baked potato and buttered spinach.

4 to 6 medium carrots
1 medium onion
1 large fresh tomato or
  2 tbsp (30 mL) tomato paste
2 tbsp (30 mL) butter
1/2 tsp (2 mL) sugar

2 tbsp (30 mL) water
a few drops tabasco
2 green onions, chopped
1/4 cup (60 mL) fresh
  parsley, chopped

Peel the carrots and cut into matchsticks. Slice the onion thinly and break into rings. Peel tomato, chop fine and mix with the sugar or blend the sugar into the tomato paste. Heat the butter in a shallow saucepan. Add the onion rings and brown lightly over medium heat. Add the tomato or tomato paste. Stir and simmer 1 minute. Stir in the carrots. Sprinkle with tabasco. Add the water. Cover and simmer 10 to 12 minutes. Salt to taste. Pour into a hot serving dish and sprinkle the top with parsley and green onion mixed together. Serves 4 to 6.

GOLDEN MAPLE GLAZED CARROTS

A perfect recipe to use with spring carrots, and fresh maple syrup. In the winter, I cut the carrots into thin matchsticks. Serve them with chicken or duck.

6 to 8 carrots
1/2 cup (125 mL) orange
  juice
grated rind of 1 orange

3 tbsp (50 mL) butter
1/4 cup (60 mL) maple syrup
  or corn syrup
a pinch of mace or coriander

Scrape the carrots or brush clean with a stiff brush. Leave whole or cut in two. Heat the orange juice with the grated rind. Add the carrots. Stir until well coated with the orange juice. Cover and cook over low heat for 10 to 15 minutes or until the carrots are tender. Add the rest of the ingredients. Uncover and cook over medium heat, stirring often with a rubber spatula, until the syrup is thick and coats the carrots. Roll in chives or parsley if you wish and serve. Serves 6.

CHESTER MASHED RED AND WHITE CARROTS

A few years ago, I spent some time vacationing in Nova Scotia. In Chester, I was served this very tasty dish made with carrots, the lady called the parsnips "white carrots."

4 to 5 carrots
3 parsnips
1/2 cup (125 mL) hot water
1/3 cup (80 mL) melted
  butter
1 tbsp (15 mL) lemon juice

1/4 cup (60 mL) fresh cream
  or sour cream
grated rind of 1 lemon
salt and pepper to taste
chopped parsley or chives

Peel the carrots and the parsnips. Cut each into thick slices. Stir together in a saucepan the hot water, melted butter and lemon juice. Add the prepared vegetables. Stir until well mixed together. Cover and simmer over medium low heat for 20 minutes. Strain, but reserve any liquid remaining (sometimes it is all evaporated, depending on the natural water content of the vegetables). Add the cream or sour cream and lemon rind to the vegetables. Mash together, and make as smooth as possible. Salt and pepper to taste. Add parsley or chives, and some of the reserved liquid, if necessary. Serve hot. Serves 6.

VARIETY IN CUCUMBERS

Cucumbers go with practically everything, cold meats, ham, chicken, steak, stew, omelet, soup, salad and so on, with fish they are not only superlative but a must. They can be creamed, fried, boiled, stuffed, made into golden fritters, mousse, cold soup and when combined in a salad with sour cream, a perfect team if blended together.

BUTTER FRIED CUCUMBERS

The first time I ate fried cucumber was in England, served piping hot with a garnish of ice cold Devonshire cream on the side. In Canada, I use sour cream.

2 tbsp (30 mL) butter
2 medium-sized cucumbers
1/4 cup (60 mL) flour
1/2 tsp (2 mL) salt

1/2 tsp (2 mL) curry powder
  (optional)
4 tbsp (60 mL) finely
  chopped parsley

Peel the cucumbers and slice them 1/2-inch (1.5-cm) thick. Dry the slices by wrapping them in absorbent paper for a few minutes. Then shake in a bag containing the flour, salt and curry powder.

Place the butter in a large frying pan and melt it. Add the floured cucumber slices, fry about 3 minutes on each side for a golden color. Do not overcook. Serve as soon as ready, sprinkled with the parsley. Serves 4.

MARTA'S FINNISH CUCUMBER SALAD

Finnish women have a way with cucumber. This salad and the cucumber sauce are two classics of their cuisine.

4 medium-sized cucumbers
1 tbsp (15 mL) chopped fresh
  or dried dill
1/2 cup (125 mL) white wine
  or cider vinegar

1/2 cup (125 mL) water
3 tbsp (50 mL) sugar
1 tsp (5 mL) salt
2 tbsp (30 mL) salad oil

Peel the cucumbers and slice paper thin. Place attractively in a semi-shallow glass dish or bowl. Sprinkle all over with the chopped dill. Stir together the vinegar, water, sugar, salt and salad oil. Pour over the cucumbers. Do not stir. Cover and refrigerate at least 2 hours, when possible, 4 hours, to allow the flavors to blend. Serve without blending. Serves 6.

AROUND THE GLOBE WITH THE CUCUMBER

— Pickle the **Gurka** - Swedish for cucumber - the way they do. Three large cucumbers thinly sliced, unpeeled, combine with 1 large Spanish onion thinly sliced and broken into rings. Then add 1/2 cup (125 mL) vinegar, parsley, dill, pepper, salt and a tablespoon (15 mL) of sugar. Toss and toss together. Chill 4 to 6 hours.

— Toss your **Kheera** - Indian for cucumber - with yoghurt for a delicious hors d'oeuvre or salad or winter garnish to your curry table. Pare 2 cucumbers, cut into small squares. Sprinkle with 1 tablespoon (15 mL) salt. Let stand 1 hour. Drain and add to the following yoghurt mixture. Combine 2 tablespoons (30 mL) parsley, crushed garlic to taste, cayenne or Tabasco to taste, 3 tablespoons (50 mL) lemon juice with 2 cups (500 mL) yoghurt.

— Make a **Gurkensalat** - German for cucumber salad - by removing each end of 4 cucumbers. Run the tines of a fork down the length of the cucumbers to form ridges. Slice thinly. Toss with 1 1/2 cups (375 mL) dairy sour cream, 1/4 cup (60 mL) cider vinegar, 1 teaspoon (5 mL) pepper, salt and minced chives to taste. Refrigerate, covered, for 1 hour.

— For a good old Canadian standby: stuff fresh pink summer tomatoes with diced cucumber and celery blended with mayonnaise, chives and parsley.

POTATOES

FOIL WRAPPED POTATOES FINES HERBES

If you like your baked potatoes moist, wrap them; if you like to eat the crips crunchy skin, prepare the same way but do not wrap.

Scrub with a stiff brush and dry potatoes of uniform size. Rub all over with melted butter, oil or beef dripping (the best). The fat will give flavor as well as keep the skin a little softer. Wrap in foil, overlapping the ends of foil. Bake in a 425°F (215°C) oven 50 to 70 minutes, depending on the size. Serve with a bowl of **fines herbes** butter.

Melt 4 tablespoons (60 mL) of butter, add 2 tablespoons (30 mL) of sour cream or rich cream, a pinch of tarragon, a tablespoon (15 mL) of minced parsley, a finely minced green onion or chives to taste, salt and pepper. Stir well together and serve as soon as hot.

POTATOES POLONAISE

One of my husband's favorite light meals. Crisp celery or a green lettuce is all that is needed to make a well balanced meal. Also very nice served with roasted chicken or poached fish.

6 medium potatoes	3 tbsp (50 mL) sour cream
3 to 4 tbsp (50 to 60 mL) bacon fat or salad oil	2 eggs
2 cups (500 mL) cottage cheese	1/4 cup (60 mL) parsley, minced
	salt and pepper to taste

Peel potatoes and slice as thinly as possible. Heat the bacon fat or oil in a large frying pan. Pour in the potatoes and stir once in a while, over medium heat, until golden brown and crisp, this will take about 15 minutes. Turn into a baking dish. Mix together the rest of the ingredients and pour over the potatoes. Bake in a 250°F (120°C) oven for 20 to 25 minutes or until the cheese is set. Serves 6.

GRILLED POTATOES

Nice with panfried or grilled meat. A useful recipe because the potatoes can be cooked ahead of time.

6 medium-sized potatoes
1/4 cup (60 mL) melted
  butter or margarine
1/4 tsp (1 mL) paprika

small bowl of coarse salt
pepper grinder
dish of unsalted butter

Scrub and boil the potatoes in their skins. Cool and peel. Cut them in half, lengthwise, place on baking sheet. Brush generously each half with the melted butter mixed with the paprika. Put under direct heat, about 2 to 3 inches (5 to 7.5 cm) away from the source of heat, grill until they are golden brown. Serve as soon as ready, with the coarse salt, pepper and unsalted butter. Let everyone use these at his discretion. Serves 6.

POTATOES GRÊLÉES

A butter fried potato coated with coarse salt or fresh breadcrumbs. Crisp and so good. Family fare in French Pays Basque.

6 to 8 medium-small potatoes
4 tbsp (60 mL) butter
3 to 4 tbsp (50 to 60 mL)
  fresh white breadcrumbs

2 tbsp (30 mL) parsley,
  minced

Scrub the new potatoes and do not peel. Wash and peel old potatoes.

Melt the butter in a heavy metal frying pan, just big enough to hold the potatoes, all in one layer. Put in the potatoes, cover the pan and cook over low heat, turning the potatoes several times during the cooking, cook until they are golden all over. Add the breadcrumbs and shake the pan over medium heat until the breadcrumbs absorb the butter and become crisp. This will take just a few minutes.

If you like coarse salt with your potatoes, replace the breadcrumbs with 1 teaspoon (5 mL) coarse salt and proceed the same way. Serves 6.

MY BEST MASHED POTATOES AND VARIATIONS

Through the years I have tried many ways of preparing mashed potatoes. These are my winners, very smooth, no lumps, creamy and enriched with instant skim milk. I prefer to pressure cook my potatoes, but they can also be boiled.

**8 potatoes, peeled and cut
in half
4 tbsp (60 mL) instant
skim milk
1/2 cup (125 mL) sour cream**

**1/4 teaspoon (1 mL) savory
1 green onion, minced
(optional)
salt and pepper to taste**

Boil the potatoes until tender, drain and put pan back over heat until the potatoes are dry. Then put through a potato ricer over the hot pan used to cook and dry the potatoes. Add the rest of the ingredients and beat until light, white and smooth. Serves 6.

Variations:

To serve with roast pork or sausages: add 2 cups (500 mL) of cooked mashed turnips to the above recipe, replace savory with sage. To serve with chicken, fish and eggs: add 1 1/2 cups (375 mL) cooked, mashed carrots to the above and replace savory with basil.

To serve with lamb, beef and hamburgers: add 1 cup (250 mL) of bacon fried onion to the above recipe. Use the savory as flavoring and add to the above recipe.

OLD FASHIONED POTATO SALAD

This potato salad has perfect keeping quality and is most tasty. The oil dressing is mine. The cooked dressing is my mother's recipe. I learned to make it from my Grand-mère. It truly makes this salad an old-fashioned family recipe.

5 to 6 cups (1.2 to 1.5 L)
  diced cooked potatoes
1 tsp (5 mL) salt
1/4 tsp (1 mL) freshly
  ground pepper
1/4 tsp (1 mL) dry mustard
generous pinch of tarragon

bit of garlic powder
  (optional)
1 tbsp (15 mL) fresh lemon
  juice
3 tbsp (50 mL) salad oil
1 cup (250 mL) celery, diced
"Grand-mère" dressing
crisp lettuce or watercress

Place the diced potatoes in a large bowl. Blend together in a bottle the salt, pepper, dry mustard, tarragon, garlic powder, fresh lemon juice and salad oil. Pour over the potatoes. Toss gently, cover the bowl. Leave 2 hours on kitchen counter. Add the celery and 1/2 cup (125 mL) or so of Grand-mère's cooked dressing. Mix lightly. Serve in a nest of lettuce or watercress. Serves 6 to 8.

GRAND-MÈRE'S COOKED DRESSING

Will keep 4 to 8 weeks in glass jar, covered and refrigerated. Nice with all types of vegetable salads.

3 tbsp (50 mL) butter
2 tbsp (30 mL) all purpose
  flour
1 1/2 tsp (7 mL) salt
1 tsp (5 mL) dry mustard
1 tbsp (15 mL) sugar
sprinkling of mace or nutmeg

1 1/4 cups (310 mL) milk or
  cream
2 egg yolks
1/3 cup (80 mL) cider vinegar
  (no other type of vinegar)
1/2 an onion, peeled

Place the butter in a heavy metal saucepan and melt it. Mix in the flour, salt, mustard, sugar and mace or nutmeg. Blend completely in the butter and add 1 cup (250 mL) of the milk. Cook over low heat, stirring most of the time, until mixture is slightly thickened and creamy. Beat the remaining 1/4 cup (60 mL) milk with the egg yolks. Stir into the hot mixture beating well as they are added. When well mixed, add the remaining ingredients. Simmer over low heat, until thickened. When cooled, remove the onion slice. Refrigerate. Yield: 1 1/2 cups (375 mL).

TOMATOES

This fruit or vegetable can be cooked in a myriad of ways: stuffed and baked, fried, scalloped, incorporated into sauces, used for flavoring, served in and as salads, even as jam.

TOMATO CONCASSÉ

This sauce has nothing French, in spite of its name. It is a specialty of Sweden. Use it on fresh trout or salmon, rice and omelettes.

6 to 8 fresh ripe tomatoes
1 small onion, chopped fine
2 tbsp (30 mL) salad oil
1 clove garlic, crushed
1 tbsp (15 mL) parsley,
  chopped fine

1/4 tsp (1 mL) tarragon
1/4 tsp (1 mL) fresh dill or
  dill seeds
1/2 tsp (2 mL) sugar or
  honey

Place the tomatoes in a bowl, pour boiling water over, let stand 3 minutes and start peeling. Cut in half and squeeze out the juice and seeds, discard. Chop the tomatoes coarsely. Fry the onion in a saucepan in the oil, until golden brown, here and there. Add the tomatoes, garlic, parsley, tarragon, dill and sugar or honey. Mix well. Cover and simmer over low heat for 20 to 25 minutes. Taste for seasoning. Do not boil or overcook because it is the slow simmering of this sauce that gives it its quality. Makes 4 portions.

TOMATOES PROVENÇALES

Simple, pungent, colorful, unforgettable.

4 large (2 lbs [1 kg]) tomatoes	1 tbsp (15 mL) sugar
3 tbsp (50 mL) olive or salad oil	1 clove garlic, crushed
1/2 tsp (2 mL) each salt and pepper	1 tbsp (15 mL) parsley, chopped
	1 tsp (5 mL) basil
	2 tbsp coarse breadcrumbs

Halve tomatoes crosswise and remove seeds by pressing each half in your hand.

Heat the oil in a large frying pan. Place tomatoes in oil cut side down, cook over medium heat about 3 minutes. Turn, sprinkle cut side with salt, pepper, and sugar mixed together. Place garlic in the bottom of pan and cook another two minutes or until the tomatoes are tender.

Remove tomatoes to a heated service platter, sprinkle the tops with parsley and basil mixed together.

Add breadcrumbs to frying pan and stir constantly over high heat until golden brown, sprinkle over tomatoes and serve. Serves 8.

FRESH STEWED TOMATOES

In the winter I use a large can of tomatoes, but the joy of fresh stewed tomatoes with slices of cold roasted chicken and toasted French bread is a must come the nice season.

12 medium-sized fresh tomatoes	1/4 tsp (1 mL) freshly ground pepper
2 thick slices bread, toasted	1 bay leaf
1 tbsp (15 mL) butter	1/4 tsp (1 mL) thyme
1 onion, chopped fine	1/4 cup (60 mL) chopped parsley
1 tbsp (15 mL) sugar	

← *Tomatoes Provençales*

Place the tomatoes in a bowl, cover with boiling water. Let stand 2 minutes, pour out the water and place in a bowl of cold water. Peel and quarter them.

Remove the crust from the toasted bread, dice and set aside. Melt 1 tablespoon (15 mL) of butter in a saucepan, add the onion and cook until it is well softened. Add the tomatoes, sugar and pepper. Bring to a boil and add the diced bread. Cover and simmer 10 minutes. Add the bay leaf, thyme and parsley. Uncover and simmer over low heat for 1 hour. The tomatoes will then be thick and creamy. Salt to taste. These stewed tomatoes reheat very well. Simmer, do not boil, when reheating. Serves 6.

PEAS AND BEANS

GREEN PEAS À LA FRANÇAISE

This is so good that I usually double the recipe and serve it for lunch with crispy French bread and thin slices of Gouda cheese.

3 tbsp (50 mL) butter
2 white onions
1 medium head lettuce

2-3 lb (1 kg-1 1/2 kg) fresh
    green peas
1/2 tsp (2 mL) sugar
4 sprigs parsley

Melt the butter in the electric frypan set at 300°F (150°C). Add minced onions. Cover and simmer without browning until soft and transparent. Reserve the outer green leaves of the lettuce whole, and place the rest, shredded, on top of the onions. Shell the green peas and place on top of the lettuce. Sprinkle with the sugar and cover with reserved lettuce leaves. Cover and lower the heat to 200°F

Cook 25 - 35 minutes, depending on the size of the peas. When done, remove the lettuce leaves, season to taste, add a piece of butter and a bit of lemon juice. Mix and garnish with the parsley. Serves 6.

GREEN BEANS REPERTOIRE

Fresh or frozen green beans usually taste better a little underdone rather than limp and overcooked. To cook ahead of time, place them in a saucepan with a pinch of sugar and pour boiling water on top, do not cover, boil fast. Drain, place in a bowl, cover with ice cubes and refrigerate 2 to 12 hours. Then reheat with only the liquid that clings to them over medium heat and they are ready to be served in seconds.

Variations for the repertoire

— Brown sliced almonds in butter, add a few drops of cider vinegar and pour over the hot beans. — Sauté a handful of dry breadcrumbs in butter with a piece of garlic or a bit of minced green onion. Pour over the beans.

— Slice fresh mushrooms, stir them in salad oil or butter over quick heat for a few seconds, add a sprinkling of tarragon and stir gently into cooked beans.

— Add a teaspoon (5 mL) of prepared horseradish to melted butter. Blend into the cooked beans.

— Try it the Italian way: stir a piece of butter in the cooked beans until it melts, add fresh lemon juice to taste. Place into the hot service dish and sprinkle with Parmesan.

— Save a cupful (250 mL) of stewed fresh tomatoes and blend with the cooked green beans.

— Boil them with a pinch of savory. Drain, flavor with lemon juice, minced fresh dill and butter.

— Blend them with fried onions and chili sauce.

EGGPLANTS

RATATOUILLE NIÇOISE

Anyone who has travelled through the South of France has enjoyed this usual cooked vegetable salad. Equally good hot or cold. Will keep 10 to 15 days refrigerated. Try it with barbecued steak or chicken.

1/2 cup (125 mL) salad oil
2 large onions, thinly sliced
2 to 3 cloves garlic, minced
1 small eggplant, peeled and diced
4 tomatoes, peeled and diced

1 small squash or zucchini, peeled and diced
2 green peppers, cleaned and diced
1/2 tsp (2 mL) basil
1/4 tsp (1 mL) thyme
salt and pepper to taste

Heat the oil in a heavy saucepan (when possible use enamel cast iron). Add the onions and garlic, brown quickly over high heat. Add the eggplant and the tomatoes. Mix all together, crushing the mixture with the back of a wooden spoon. Add the squash or zucchini, and the green peppers. Mix well. Add the rest of the ingredients. Cook for 2 to 3 minutes over high heat, stirring most of the time.

Cover and simmer 1 hour, over low heat, stirring once or twice. It is ready when the sauce is thick and creamy. The ratatouille is served hot or cold, as a hors d'oeuvre, a salad or a vegetable. When serving cold, sprinkle with the juice of 1/2 to 1 lemon. Taste for seasoning. Serves 6.

VEGETARIAN CURRY

The aim of the curry eater is to savor his food. The flavor is therefore all important and this curry has a lot, it reheats beautifully, costs little to make, and brings more vegetables into one's diet.

1 medium-sized eggplant
4 medium-sized potatoes
4 carrots
2 tsp (10 mL) turmeric
1/2 tsp (2 mL) ground ginger
1-inch (2.5-cm) cinnamon
  stick, broken up
seeds of 3 cardamom pods
1 tsp (5mL) ground cumin
1 to 3 garlic cloves, crushed
3 dry chili peppers
2 sliced onions
1 tbsp (15 mL) butter

grated flesh of 1 fresh coconut
  or 1/2 lb (250 g) unsweetened
  dessicated coconut
1/4 cup (60 mL) minced green
  or Italian parsley
2 cups (500 mL) hot water
2 onions, peeled and cut in
  halves
1/2 lb (250 g) green peas or
  green beans
2 cups (500 mL) canned
  tomatoes

Peel the eggplant, potatoes and carrots. Cut into thick slices, cover with cold water and set aside. Blend together the turmeric, ginger, cinnamon, coriander, cardamom, cumin, garlic and dry chili peppers. Add a little water to make a sort of paste with small pieces in it.

Heat the butter in a saucepan, add the spice mixture and fry for a second or two over medium heat, stirring all the time. Add the sliced onions and keep stirring for another minute. Add the coconut and mix thoroughly. Add the parsley, hot water and onions, then add the eggplant, potatoes and carrots well drained.

Bring to a boil and add the green peas or beans and the canned tomatoes. Cover and simmer over low heat until the vegetables are tender, about 25 to 30 minutes. Uncover and cook over high heat until most of the liquid evaporates, leaving a rich thick gravy, this happens fairly quickly in 6 to 10 minutes, and so watch closely for the right texture. Serve with plain boiled rice and sour pickles. Superb with all barbecued meats as a vegetable dish. Serves 6.

A FEW APPETIZERS

GREEN BUTTER DIP

Avocado is often referred to in the South as vegetable butter. Buy underripe fruit and ripen at room temperature. Ripe fruit yields to gentle pressure.

1 1/2 cups (375 mL) mashed
  ripe avocado
juice of 2 limes or 1 lemon
grated rind of either fruit

salt and pepper to taste
a few drops of Tabasco or
  cayenne

Mash the avocado with a fork. Thoroughly blend with the other ingredients. Refrigerate tightly covered. Yield: about 1 1/2 cups (375 mL).

BLUE CHEESE CROCK

A crock is usually a cheese blended with herbs and brandy, served on its own or as part of a hors d'oeuvres table, to be spread on crisp bread or biscuits.

1/4 lb (125 g) blue cheese
  (Danish, Italian or French)
1/2 cup (125 mL) soft butter
1 small clove garlic, crushed

1 tbsp (15 mL) parsley,
  finely chopped
2 green onions, finely chopped
3 tbsp (50 mL) brandy

Have the cheese and butter at room temperature. Place in a bowl, add the remaining ingredients and blend thoroughly by hand or with an electric mixer. Pack into a small earthenware or porcelain jar. Cover and refrigerate.

The mixture may also be shaped into a roll and dipped in toasted sesame seeds or chopped walnuts or parsley.

VEGETABLES À LA GRECQUE

Greece's favorite hors d'oeuvre, the secret of its flavor is the sauce in which the vegetables are cooked, and marinate for an hour or 2 days.

2 cups (500 mL) water or
   white wine
1/2 cup (125 mL) olive or
   salad oil
juice of 1 lemon
1 tsp (5 mL) salt

1/2 tsp (2 mL) pepper
1 bay leaf
1 tsp (5 mL) thyme
1 tsp (5 mL) crushed
   coriander seeds
2 cloves garlic, cut in four

Combine all ingredients in a saucepan, large enough to accommodate vegetable to be cooked. Add the vegetable of your choice (1 to 2 lb [500 g to 1 kg]), bring sauce to a boil, over high heat, then reduce heat and simmer uncovered until tender, being careful not to allow the vegetable to become soft and mushy.

Pour into a glass dish. Cool. Cover and keep refrigerated. Serve in its sauce or drained.

Best vegetables to prepare à la grecque

Small French artichokes, left whole; Jerusalem artichokes, peeled and sliced; Asparagus, whole or cut in 2-inch (5 cm) pieces; Green beans, whole or diced; Carrots, sliced in rounds or matchsticks; Cauliflower, divided into flowerets; Eggplant, peeled and cubed; Mushrooms, preferably small (for mushrooms reduce liquid to 1 cup (250 mL), increase oil to ¾ cup (90 mL); Small white onions, left whole; Zucchini, unpeeled and sliced.

LACE POTATO CRISPS

Make a week ahead. Cool. Wrap and freeze. To serve place frozen, one next to the other, on a baking sheet. Warm up in a preheated 400°F (200°C) oven 10 to 12 minutes or until piping hot. Serve hot on a silver tray with small finger napkins.

1 large peeled potato, grated   **1/4 tsp (1 mL) savory**
1 medium-sized onion, grated   **salad oil**
1/4 tsp (1 mL) salt

Grate and mix together the potato and the onion. Add the salt and savory.

Heat salad oil in an iron frying pan to sizzling hot. Drop the mixture by small spoonfuls into the hot oil. They cook quickly, about 30 seconds on each side, and they are most attractive, all lacy, crisp and golden brown.

TERRINE DE CAMPAGNE

A terrine is a meat loaf with personality. A slice of this pâté served with crusty French bread and a glass of light red wine is indeed an elegant hors d'oeuvre.

1 lb (500 g) lamb or pork
  liver
1 cup (250 mL) chopped
  onions
2 garlic cloves, crushed
1/4 cup (60 mL) brandy
2/3 cup (160 mL) port wine
1/4 lb (125 g) each ground
  veal and pork

1 1/2 tsp (7 mL) salt
1/2 tsp (2 mL) pepper
1 bay leaf
1 tsp (5 mL) each tarragon
  and thyme
2 eggs, beaten
strips of side bacon

With a sharp knife, coarsely chop the liver (don't grind it) and place in a non-metal bowl with the onion, garlic, brandy and port. Cover and refrigerate 24 hours to marinate. Add remaining ingredients except bacon and mix thoroughly (an electric mixer can be used at medium speed for 5 minutes).

Line a terrine or an 8 x 5-inch (20 x 12.5-cm) loaf pan with strips of bacon. Pour in meat mixture, place in a pan of hot water and bake uncovered in a 350°F (180°C) oven for 1 hour. Turn heat to 300°F (150°C) and bake 30 minutes.

Remove from oven, cover with foil or waxed paper and place a heavy object on top - the chefs use a brick, but a can of tomatoes or some such thing can replace it. Refrigerate 12 hours, then unmold. A terrine will keep 2 - 3 weeks refrigerated, 2 months frozen. This will serve 12.

Variations: Replace the veal and pork with an equal amount of raw wild or domestic duck. Or when marinating the liver, add 1/2 lb (250 g) of coarsely chopped venison, sliced raw pheasant or partridge breasts. Make terrine as indicated, layering thin slices of pheasant or partridge between liver mixture. The baking time remains the same.

Soups

SOUPS

HOT AND COLD

CREATE-YOUR-OWN COLD SOUP

Here are a few soups that require no heating at all and only a few seconds of preparation. You may create your own soups by merely blending and flavoring 2 or 3 types of canned soups and beating them in the blender for 30 seconds, or by hand until well mixed.

1 can cream of chicken soup
1 can cream of mushroom
  soup
1 soup can of milk
1/2 can water
1 tbsp (15 mL) lemon juice
1/2 tsp (2 mL) tarragon or
  1/2 cup (125 mL) diced
  cooked chicken

1 can cream of celery soup
1 can cream of tomato soup
1 can lobster paste
pinch of curry
2 cups (500 mL) milk
1 cup (250 mL) light cream

1 can cream of tomato soup
1 can cream of celery soup
1 soup can of milk
1/2 soup can of light cream
1/4 cup (60 mL) finely diced
  celery

QUICK JELLIED MADRILÈNE

A true Madrilène is much more involved. This one is good and quick although not as delicate.

2 envelopes unflavored
  gelatin
1/2 cup (125 mL) cold water
2 cups (500 mL) tomato juice
2 cups (500 mL) consommé
  or stock
1 small onion, grated

1/2 cup (125 mL) celery
  leaves, minced
1/2 tsp (2 mL) basil
1 tsp (5 mL) sugar
1 tsp (5 mL) coarse salt
1 tbsp (15 mL) lemon juice

Soak the gelatin in the cold water for 5 minutes. Bring the remaining ingredients to a boil. Boil for 2 minutes. Remove from heat, add the gelatine while stirring to dissolve it completely. Strain through a damp cloth. Refrigerate for the bouillon to jell.

To serve, break up the jelly with a fork, place in cups and garnish with a slice of lemon, sprinkle with paprika. Serves 5 - 6.

SUMMER BORSCH

Make this the day before you want to serve it. It looks most appetizing when served in white or pink bowls — they will enhance its deep purple color.

2 cups (500 mL) chopped
  canned beets
1 can undiluted beef bouillon
1 tsp (5 mL) green onions,
  chopped

1 cup (250 mL) cold water
salt and pepper to taste
2 tbsp (30 mL) lemon juice
1/3 cup (80 mL) sour cream

Drain the beets thoroughly before chopping, and reserve the liquid. Heat the beet juice, bouillon, onions and water until boiling, then add the salt, pepper and lemon juice and mix well. Add the chopped beets and pour the whole into a bowl. Cool and refrigerate.

Just before serving, top each bowl of borsch with a generous portion of sour cream. Serves 4.

NO-WORK VICHYSSOISE

Peeling and cooking onions is the only work involved in making this.
Serve it cold, topped with minced chives or grated cucumber.

4 thickly sliced onions	**2 cans frozen potato soup**
1 1/2 cups (375 mL) water	**2 cans chicken with rice soup**
1/4 tsp (1 mL) sugar	**1 cup (250 mL) cream**

Combine the onions, water and sugar and boil over medium heat for
10 minutes. Add the potato and chicken with rice soups and heat
thoroughly. Pass the soup through a food mill or sieve, then add the
cream. Cover and refrigerate until ready to serve. Serves 5 - 6.

COLD PINK SOUP

A summer soup of distinction. Just shake and serve.

juice of 1 lemon	**1 can milk**
6 ice cubes	**pinch of basil**
1 can tomato soup	

Squeeze the lemon juice over the ice cubes in a glass jug or shaker, add
the tomato soup, milk and basil. Shake until blended and frothy. Enjoy!
Serves 4.

CHILLED TOMATO-AND-CUCUMBER

Quick, easy and so refreshing.

1 can tomato soup
1/2 cucumber, grated
1 soup can water
1/4 cup (60 mL) green
   onions, chopped
1 tsp (5 mL) Worcestershire
   sauce

1 tsp (5 mL) salt
1/8 tsp (0.5 mL) pepper
chopped parsley
1/2 cup (125 mL) heavy
   cream

To the tomato soup add the cucumber, water, green onions, Worcestershire sauce, salt and pepper. Chill for several hours. Strain. Add the
cream. Chill. Garnish with chopped parsley. Serves 4.

60-SECOND SENEGALESE

This delightful soup takes only 30 seconds to make in a blender and 60
seconds by hand. It's real joy, considering that the original recipe takes
hours to prepare.

1 can cream of chicken soup
1 soup can of milk
1 tbsp (15 mL) sour cream

1/2 tsp (2 mL) curry powder
minced chives or parsley

Combine all the ingredients, except the chives or parsley, and beat 30
seconds in the blender or 60 seconds with a hand beater. Taste for seasoning and add more curry, if you wish. Cover and refrigerate 4 - 6 hours,
then serve garnished with chives or parsley to taste. Serves 3 - 4.

CHILLED SEAFOOD BISQUE

To eat in the garden on a hot sunny day.

1 can tomato soup
1 can milk
1 can (4 1/2 oz [113 mL])
  small shrimp
1 can (6 1/2 oz [198 mL])
  crabmeat

1/2 cup (125 mL) red wine
salt and pepper
lemon juice
chopped chives

Beat the tomato soup and milk until smooth. Add the shrimps, drained; the crabmeat, flaked; and the red wine. Season to taste with salt, pepper, lemon juice. Chill. Sprinkle with chopped chives and serve. Serves 4.

GREEN CHICKEN SOUP

The main ingredients for this colorful and tasty, hot or cold soup are a box of frozen spinach and a couple of cans of soup.

1 pkg frozen spinach
2 cans cream of chicken soup
1 soup can of milk
1/2 crushed garlic clove
pinch of cayenne

2 tbsp (30 mL) sour or
  whipped cream
freshly ground pepper, to
  taste

Defrost the spinach, then place it in a saucepan with the rest of the ingredients. Bring to a boil over medium heat, stirring often.

Beat with a hand beater or wire whisk until creamy, then serve **hot or cold** garnished with a teaspoon (5 mL) of sour or whipped cream and freshly ground pepper. Serves 5 - 6.

POTAGE ST.GERMAIN

Often made with green split peas, but the true St.Germain is made with fresh green peas, or if necessary, frozen green peas. Equally good hot or cold.

3 cups (750 mL) shelled fresh peas (about 3 lb [1 kg 1/2])
or
3 cups (750 mL) frozen green peas
2 Boston or large Bibb lettuce

2 small leeks, cleaned and sliced
4 cups (1 L) water
salt to taste
2 tbsp (30 mL) butter
1/2 cup (125 mL) rich or light cream

Place in saucepan the shelled fresh peas or frozen peas, the lettuce coarsely shredded and the leeks. Add the water and salt. Bring to boil, then cook over medium heat until peas are tender: 15 minutes for fresh peas, 10 minutes for frozen peas. Then drain the vegetables and reserve the liquid.

Pass the vegetables through a strainer or a **presse-purée**. Return the purée to the saucepan and thin to the desired consistency with the reserved liquid. Bring back to a boil, then add gradually the butter and the cream, while beating constantly. Taste for seasoning and serve at once. To serve cold, omit the butter and add the cream when ready to serve. Serves 4 to 6.

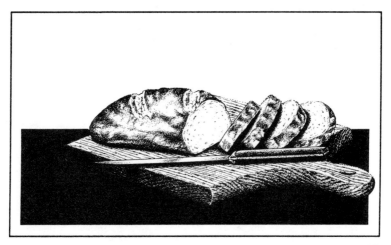

BEEF STOCK OR BOUILLON

A good stock is the basis for hundreds of delectable soups, sauces and other dishes. Although the preparation is a bit time consuming, it is not complicated, and you let it simmer slowly without having to watch it. It will keep from two to three weeks refrigerated — six to seven months frozen.

2 tbsp (30 mL) beef fat
  or butter
2 lb (1 kg) brisket or
  shoulder of beef
1 to 2 lb (500 g to 1 kg) veal
  knuckle
3 quarts (3.7 L) tepid water

4 medium onions, quartered
2 whole carrots
3 whole cloves
1 tbsp (15 mL) coarse salt
1/2 tsp (2 mL) dry mustard
1/2 tsp (2 mL) thyme
1 cup (250 mL) celery leaves,
  chopped

Melt the beef fat or butter in a soup kettle, and brown beef in it. Add the remaining ingredients. Bring to a boil. Skim. Cover and simmer over low heat for 2 1/2 hours.

To strain the consommé, when cooked, spread a damp cloth over a large bowl. Empty the contents of the soup kettle into the cloth. Let it drain without touching, it takes but a few seconds. Pour into bottles, cover and refrigerate. When the consommé cools, the fat will rise to the top and harden, which prevents air from penetrating and the consommé may be kept, refrigerated, from 2 to 3 weeks. The cooled consommé is jellied. Yield: 3 quarts (3.7 L).

CHICKEN CONSOMMÉ

Use the cooked chicken meat for salad or chicken pie. As it is difficult to find a truly good chicken consommé, I recommend keeping some on hand. It will keep refrigerated or frozen for same amount of time as basic beef consommé.

4 lb (2 kg) boiling fowl	**1/2 bay leaf**
butter	**1/4 tsp (1 mL) peppercorns**
6 cups (1.5 L) cold water	**1/4 tsp (1 mL) thyme**
1 carrot, sliced	**1 tbsp (15 mL) coarse salt**
2 stalks celery	**1 onion, finely minced**
1 clove garlic, chopped	

Cut up the chicken and brown the pieces lightly in a little butter. Transfer to a soup kettle and add the remaining ingredients. Cover and bring to a boil. Simmer for 1 1/2 to 2 hours or until the chicken is tender.

Strain the same way as the basic beef consommé. Keep refrigerated. Yield: 6 cups (1.5 L) consommé.

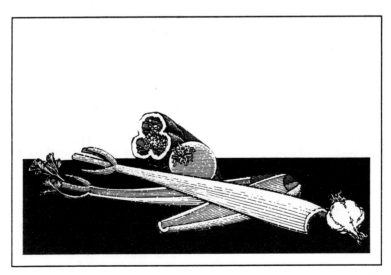

EGG SOUP

An excellent soup to serve at a dinner party — it is taken from the Italian cuisine.

4 cups (1 L) chicken or beef
  consommé
2 whole eggs
1 1/2 tbsp (22 mL) flour

2 tbsp (30 mL) Parmesan
  cheese, grated
minced chives or parsley

Bring the chicken or beef consommé to a boil. Place in a bowl the eggs, flour, grated cheese. Beat with a fork until well blended.

Slowly add egg mixture to hot chicken broth, stirring constantly to shred eggs. Simmer 5 minutes over low heat. Serve topped with minced chives or parsley. Serves 4.

CREAM OF CORN SOUP

This nourishing, easy-to-prepare soup is especially good garnished with crumbled bacon, or peanuts browned in butter. For a thicker soup, use cream-style corn, for a lighter soup, use corn kernels.

1 onion, chopped
1 celery stalk, diced
  (optional)
1/4 cup (60 mL)
  margarine or 3 tbsp (50 mL)
  bacon fat

1/4 cup (60 mL) flour
4 cups (1 L) milk
15-oz (255-mL) can corn
1/4 tsp (1 mL) curry powder
salt and pepper to taste

Sauté the onion and celery in the margarine or bacon fat just until the onion is lightly browned. Then add the flour and blend the whole thoroughly.

Add the milk, stir until thickened, then add the corn, curry powder, salt and pepper. Mix well, cover and leave over very low heat until ready to serve. Serves 6.

TOMATO SOUP "DE MA TANTE"

I have never tasted a better fresh tomato soup than this one, which was the delight of my younger days and still is. My aunt always used fresh basil to flavor the soup.

**24 medium-sized sweet
   red tomatoes
1 tbsp (15 mL) sugar
2 tbsp (30 mL) butter
1 onion, quartered
2 bay leaves
2 celery ribs with leaves
1 tbsp (15 mL) minced fresh basil
   or crumbled dried basil**

**1 tsp (5 mL) salt
1/4 tsp (1 mL) freshly
   ground pepper
3 tbsp (50 mL) minced fresh
   parsley
juice of 1/2 a lemon
1/2 cup (125 mL) whipped
   cream.**

Cut the unpeeled tomatoes into quarters. Place in a heavy metal saucepan with the sugar, butter, onion, bay leaves, celery and basil. Cover and simmer over low heat for 30 minutes. Do not add water at any time. Pass through a food mill or a sieve. Put back in the saucepan and add the salt, pepper, parsley and lemon juice. Simmer for a few minutes. Taste for seasoning. Serve in cups, topped with a spoonful (5 mL) of whipped cream, slightly salted. Serves 8 or more.

VEGETABLE CHEESE SOUP

Especially nice for a company dinner. Serve with small bowls of grated cheese and finely chopped chives or parsley.

**2/3 cup (160 mL) carrots,
   grated
1/2 cup (125 mL) celery,
   finely diced
1/3 cup (80 mL) green
   onions, chopped
1/4 cup (60 mL) butter
1/3 cup (80 mL) flour**

**2 cups (500 mL) chicken
   bouillon or 2 cups (500 mL)
   water with 2 chicken cubes
2 cups (500 mL) light cream
   or milk
1/4 tsp (1 mL) salt
1 cup (250 mL) grated strong
   cheddar
1 tbsp (15 mL) brandy**

Place in saucepan the carrots, celery, onions and butter. Stir until well coated with the butter, then cook over low heat until soft but not browned. Blend in the flour. Stir in the bouillon or water and cubes, then the milk or cream. Cook and stir, over medium heat, until mixture comes to boil and thickens.

Add the salt, cheese and brandy. Heat just enough to melt the cheese. Serve. Yield: about 1 quart (1.2 L).

MY LENTIL SOUP

Meatless and so good. Do not reduce the butter quantity — as it replaces the protein.

2 cups (500 mL) brown
  lentils
4 cups (1 L) cold water
2 tbsp (30 mL) salt
1/4 tsp (1 mL) pepper
1/2 cup (125 mL) butter

1 large can (1 lb 13 oz [625 g])
  tomatoes
1 large onion, diced
2 tbsp (30 mL) fresh dill, or
  1 tbsp (15 mL) dill seeds
2 garlic cloves, crushed
2 bay leaves

Place all the ingredients in a saucepan. Slowly bring to a boil. Cover and simmer over low heat for 2 to 2 1/2 hours. Serves about 6.

AUVERGNE ONION SOUP

In Auvergne, it is called **la bolée**. Quick and economical to make, it has been one of my treasured recipes dating back to my student days in Paris.

6 onions, thinly sliced
1 quart (1.2 L) water
1 tsp (5 mL) salt
1/4 tsp (1 mL) pepper
pinch of thyme
4 tbsp (60 mL) farina (cream
  of wheat)

3 tbsp (50 mL) melted chicken
  fat or butter
2 egg yolks
3 tbsp (50 mL) rich or sour
  cream
1/4 tsp (1 mL) celery salt
1/4 cup (60 mL) fresh parsley,
  finely chopped

Bring the water to a full rolling boil with salt, pepper and thyme. Add the farina while beating with a whisk or rotary beater. Simmer over very low heat for 8 minutes.

Melt the chicken fat or butter, add the onions and simmer, uncovered, over low heat, until the onions are soft. Add to the water and simmer 10 minutes. (This first part can be cooked ahead of time.)

To serve, place the egg yolks in a soup tureen or earthenware casserole, add the cream and beat together until well blended. Pour the boiling hot soup on top, beating all the while. Add the celery salt and parsley. Serves 4 - 5.

In Auvergne, the 2 egg whites are cooked in a frying pan in a bit of butter. When cooked, they are cooled and sliced, or chopped, and used as a garnish on top of the soup.

CENTRAL EUROPEAN POTATO SOUP

An unusual, colorful and very tasty vegetable soup.

1 cup (250 mL) slivered
  carrots
1/4 cup (60 mL) each celery,
  parsnip, slivered
3 cups (750 mL) cubed,
  pared potatoes
2 1/2 tsp (12 mL) salt
2 quarts (2.5 L) boiling water
1 tbsp (15 mL) butter or
  margarine

1/2 lb (250 g) fresh
  mushrooms, sliced
1/2 tsp (2 mL) salt
1/4 tsp (1 mL) pepper
3 tbsp (50 mL) butter
1/4 cup (60 mL) flour
1 cup (250 mL) cold water
1 clove garlic crushed
1 tsp (1 mL) marjoram

Place in large saucepan the vegetables, potatoes, the 2 1/2 tsp (12 mL) salt, and hot water. Cover and simmer 40 minutes. Melt the 1 tablespoon (15 mL) butter in frying pan, add mushrooms and stir 3 minutes over high heat. Add to soup and simmer 10 minutes.

Melt in frying pan the 3 tablespoons (50 mL) butter, stir in the flour until smooth, continue stirring until mixture is light brown. Stir in the cold water. Mix well. Add to soup with the garlic and marjoram. Stir while simmering until the whole is well blended. Serves 6 to 8.

Desserts

DESSERTS

Some desserts belong to what I call the "dramatic group," such as souf-flés, flambés and pièces montées. They are delicate and superb, but require quite a fund of basic knowledge to succeed and they are lots of work.

Others belong to the "baking desserts": cakes, tortes, pastries, pies; these are lovely, but they also imply quite a bit of work. The ones I prefer are the light, delicate type of dessert, which usually can be prepared ahead of time. They are elegant and easy.

To sum it up, there is really only one successful dessert, the one that fits the meal that precedes it. A heavy meal demands a delicate, light dessert, like Snow Squares or Caramel Custard. Keep Green Apple Pie à la Mode for a light meal and everybody will be happy.

The simplest of all desserts is too often forgotten. A basket of perfect fruits or a platter of assorted cheeses with crisp crackers or cream cheese with homemade jams or jellies and hot muffins.

Desserts are the poetry and romance of a meal. Let's enjoy them!

ANNETTE'S CHOCOLATE CAKE

Annette had a flair for cake making. This chocolate cake was one of her masterpieces. Do not worry about the quite thin batter, that is as it shoud be. The result is a dark, full flavored chocolate cake with a sponge cake texture.

2 ounces (60 mL)
  unsweetened chocolate
1 cup (250 mL) milk
2 tbsp (30 mL) butter
1 cup (250 mL) sugar

1 egg yolk
1 cup (250 mL) all purpose
  flour
1 tsp (5 mL) soda

Melt the chocolate over very low heat in a heavy metal saucepan. Add 1/2 cup (125 mL) of the milk and stir until thick. Remove from heat. Add the butter and stir until melted. Add the sugar, mix and stir in the egg yolks. Mix thoroughly at that stage. Stir the soda with the flour and add to the chocolate mixture, alternately with the other 1/2 cup (125 mL) milk. Beat well. Pour into a greased and floured 8 x 8 x 2-inch (20 x 20 x 5-cm) cake pan. Bake at 375°F (190°C) for 30 minutes. Frost as you wish. I like mine just as is. Yield: 9 servings.

BUTTER FROSTING AND VARIATIONS

Any of the cupcakes and cakes can be frosted and garnished to taste. It is hard to go wrong with such a good basic frosting.

1/4 cup (60 mL) butter
2 cups (500 mL) icing sugar
1/8 tsp (0.5 mL) salt

3 tbsp (50 mL) water, juice, milk or cream
1 tsp (5 mL) vanilla)

Cream the butter, add 1 cup (250 mL) of the icing sugar gradually, while stirring all the time. When very creamy start adding the second cup (250 mL) of icing sugar with the salt and alternately with the liquid of your choice. Add the vanilla and beat, adding a bit of sugar or liquid, if necessary, to have just the proper consistency.

VARIATIONS:

Chocolate Frosting: Add 1/3 cup (80 mL) cocoa, sifted with sugar, or 2 ounces (60 mL) of melted and cooled chocolate.

Coffee Frosting: Sift 2 tablespoons (30 mL) instant coffee with the sugar, use light cream as liquid.

Lemon Frosting: Use 3 tablespoons (50 mL) fresh lemon juice as liquid and 1 teaspoon (5 mL) grated lemon rind to replace the vanilla.

Orange Frosting: Same as lemon frosting replacing lemon by orange.

Maple Frosting: Replace 3 tablespoons (50 mL) liquid and the 1 teaspoon (5 mL) vanilla with an equal measure of maple syrup.

Fresh Strawberry Frosting: Crush enough fresh strawberries to have 1/4 cup (60 mL). Use to replace liquid and vanilla of basic recipe. When available, add 1/2 teaspoon (2 mL) rose water. A superb frosting.

PRALINE TOPPING

Mix topping 1/2 cup (125 mL) brown sugar, 1 cup (250 mL) chopped nuts, 1/4 cup (60 mL) melted butter and 3 tablespoons (50 mL) cream. Place on hot or cooled cake. Broil 3 inches (7.5 cm) from direct heat 1 to 2 minutes or until pale brown.

PINK LEMONADE FROSTING

Whip together in a bowl, with electric mixer, until thick enough to spread 1/2 cup (125 mL) frozen lemonade concentrate, plain or pink (do not dilute), 1 lb (500 g) icing sugar, 2 egg whites, a pinch of salt. Try this on a one egg or hot milk cake.

BAKER'S GLAZE FOR CAKES

Stir together 1/2 cup (125 mL) water, 1/3 cup (80 mL) corn syrup and 1 cup (250 mL) sugar. Heat slowly until sugar dissolves. Then boil until a firm ball is formed when dropped in cold water. Brush sparingly on cake while still hot. The cake can be hot or cold. Decorate to taste with cherries, nuts, etc. Glaze decorations.

WHIPPED CREAM FROSTING OR FILING

Soften 2 teaspoons (10 mL) of unflavored gelatine in 2 tablespoons (30 mL) of cream for 5 minutes. Dissolve over hot water. Cool a few minutes. Whip 2 cups (500 mL) chilled cream until stiff. Add 1/2 cup (125 mL) sugar gradually, then the gelatine, beating all the while. Beat until mixture stands in peaks. Flavor with 1/2 teaspoon (2 mL) of vanilla or 1 tablespoon (15 mL) of dry instant coffee. Frost or fill cake. Chill. The gelatine makes the cream stand up for a day.

Butter Frosting and Variations →

KENT YULETIDE CAKE

An old Kentish recipe, a superb, traditional fruit cake. It is made with self-rising flour. The longer this cake is kept, the better it is. I like to make it at least 3 weeks before Christmas.

1 cup (250 mL) unsalted butter
1 2/3 cups (410 mL) brown sugar
5 eggs
2 tsp (10 mL) molasses
1 1/2 cups (375 mL) seedless raisins
3/4 cup (190 mL) diced, mixed peel
1 1/2 cups (375 mL) currants

3/4 cup (190 mL) candied cherries
1 cup (250 mL) muscat raisins
1/2 cup (125 mL) chopped almonds
2 tbsp (30 mL) allspice
1/2 tsp (2 mL) salt
3 cups (750 mL) self-rising flour
1/3 cup (80 mL) brandy

Cream the butter and brown sugar until light. Add the eggs, one at a time, beating well at each addition. Add the molasses and beat.

In a large bowl mix the seedless raisins, mixed peel , candied cherries, currants, muscat raisins, almonds, allspice, salt and self-rising flour. Stir with your hands until well blended together.

Add to the egg mixture and again stir with your hands until very well blended. Add the brandy and mix thoroughly.

Butter a 10-inch (25-cm) cake pan, 4 inches (10 cm) deep, then line the bottom with waxed paper. Pour in the batter. Bake 3 to 3 1/2 hours in a 300°F (150°C) oven in the middle shelf.

Cool completely in the pan, set on a rack before unmolding. Remove the waxed paper.

To keep, wrap the cake in a cheesecloth dipped in brandy, and then in clear plastic wrap and foil. Refrigerate or keep in a cool place.

It will keep 12 to 16 months, refrigerated. It can be cut in four to make wedges of Christmas cake to be covered with thinly rolled almond paste. Serves 10 to 15.

← *Kent Yuletide Cake*

SNOW SQUARES

A delicate white foam topped with a daffodil yellow lemon sauce. Will keep 3 to 4 days, refrigerated.

1 envelope unflavored
  gelatine
1 tbsp (15 mL) cold water
1 1/2 cups (375 mL) hot water

1/4 cup (60 mL) lemon juice
2 egg whites
1/2 cup (125 mL) sugar
pinch of salt

Sauce:

1/2 cup (125 mL) lemon juice
1/2 cup (125 mL) orange
  juice
pinch of salt
1/2 cup (125 mL) sugar

3 tbsp (50 mL) cornstarch
2 egg yolks
1 cup (250 mL) whipping
  cream

To make the snow: Soak the gelatin in cold water for 5 minutes. Add hot water and stir until dissolved. If necessary, stir over low heat. Add the 1/4 cup (60 mL) lemon juice. Cool.

In a large bowl add the gelatin, sugar and salt to the unbeaten egg whites. Beat with an electric or rotary beater until mixture holds firm peaks when beater is removed.

Pour into a round cut-crystal bowl and chill until firm. Serve with the sauce, made as follows: place in a saucepan the lemon and orange juices; combine thoroughly in a bowl the sugar, salt and cornstarch and add to the juice while stirring. Cook over low heat, stirring all the time until thick and creamy.

Remove from heat, add a few spoonfuls of the hot mixture to the beaten egg yolks, pour back into hot mixture while stirring, cook over very low heat 1 minute, while stirring. Refrigerate until ready to serve, then fold in the cream, whipped stiff.

For a variation, decorate Snow with fresh strawberries or raspberries, sweetened with honey to taste. Serves 6 to 8.

NUTMEG PINEAPPLE SAUCE

This topping for ice cream is supreme elegance. The original hostess always reminded her guests that the fresh pineapple came "all the way from Hawaii by the fastest boat," but today you can make it as successfully with canned crushed pineapple. Try it sometimes on fresh mint sherbet.

1/4 cup (60 mL) honey
1 tbsp (15 mL) cornstarch
pinch of salt
1/4 tsp (1 mL) ground
  nutmeg

1 1/4 cups (310 mL) crushed
  pineapple
grated rind of 1 lemon
juice of 1/2 a lemon
1 tsp (5 mL) vanilla

Place in a saucepan the honey, cornstarch, salt and nutmeg. Stir until well mixed. Add the undrained pineapple, lemon rind and juice. Stir and cook over medium heat until creamy and transparent. Remove from heat, stir in vanilla. Cool. Refrigerate until ready to use over vanilla or chocolate ice cream. Serves 8 to 10.

PEAR CHARLOTTE

An old fashioned bread and fruit pudding that still has much charm. Serve it with cold rich cream.

2 cups (500 mL) pears,
  peeled and thinly sliced
grated rind and juice of
  1 orange
pinch of coriander or cloves
1/4 cup (60 mL) butter,
  melted

3 egg yolks, beaten
3 tbsp (50 mL) honey
3 tbsp (50 mL) brown sugar
2 1/2 cups (625 mL) fluffy
  fresh coarse breadcrumbs
3 egg whites

Place in a mixing bowl the pears, rind and juice of the oranges, the coriander or cloves, melted butter, egg yolks, honey and brown sugar. Mix thoroughly. Beat the egg whites until stiff, add the breadcrumbs, mixing them in gently. Fold into the pear mixture. Pour into a well buttered 8-inch (20-cm) baking dish.

Bake in a preheated 350°F (180°C) oven for 30 to 35 minutes or until well puffed and golden brown. Serves 4 to 6.

BREAD AND BUTTER PUDDING

This delicious bread pudding, so often served to my guests, has never failed to please them. It is nice just as is. For a fancy sauce that is superb, heat together, without boiling, an equal quantity each of maple syrup and brandy or rum. When hot add a tablespoon (15 mL) or so of butter. It is like a hot toddy being poured over the pudding.

**3 cups (750 mL) of light
  cream or milk
3 eggs
1 cup (250 mL) sugar
1 tsp (5 mL) vanilla**

**pinch of mace
6 slices bread, thickly
  buttered
1/2 cup (125 mL) seedless
  raisins or currants**

Scald the cream or milk. Beat the eggs with the sugar, vanilla and mace. Add to the milk, beat with rotary beater until well blended. In a thickly buttered pudding dish make alternate rows of buttered bread and raisins or currants. Pour the hot milk mixture on top. Place the dish in a pan of hot water. Bake 50 to 60 minutes in a 325°F (160°C) oven or until puffed and golden brown. Serves 6.

TWO COLD SOUFFLÉS

A cold soufflé will add delicious allure to your dessert repertoire and it will not disgrace your culinary savoir-faire by collapsing just before you bring it to the table. In appearance it resembles a hot soufflé — the effect being achieved by putting a collar on the soufflé dish, so that when the mixture is thoroughly chilled, it will be set in place. Then the collar is removed, and the soufflé is higher than the level of the dish. If you wish to achieve this effect, it is important to choose the right size of dish so that you will have enough mixture to pile high in the dish.

This is how the collar is prepared. Use a piece of waxed paper long enough to go around the outside edge of the dish and fold it in half lengthwise. Butter the inside fold which is next to the soufflé mixture. Tie with a string around the soufflé dish, so that about 2 inches (5 cm) of the paper stand above the top of the dish. When you pour the mixture into the dish, fill the dish and the paper collar to 1 1/2 inches (3.8 cm) above the top of the dish.

When you are ready to serve, remove the dish from the refrigerator, and cut the string holding the waxed paper. Pull the paper away with care. You can sprinkle the edges of the soufflé above the rim of the dish with finely chopped toasted almonds or chocolate shots or colored sugar if you wish.

It is a very practical and elegant dessert to know how to make when you have guests as it should remain 4 to 6 hours in the refrigerator, and will be even better when left overnight.

CHOCOLATE SOUFFLÉ

One of the most popular of all cold soufflés. I sometimes replace the ordinary semi-sweet chocolate by the Swiss imported type of various flavors — 150 to 200 grams weight (indicated on label) is needed to replace the 5 ounces (115 g) called for. Each type of chocolate gives a different flavor to the soufflé.

2 envelopes unflavored
  gelatin
1/4 cup (60 mL) rum or
  orange juice
5 (1 ounce [27 mL] each)
  squares semi-sweet chocolate
2/3 cup (160 mL) milk

5 egg yolks
2/3 cup (160 mL) sugar
1 tsp (5 mL) vanilla
1 1/2 cups (375 mL) heavy
  cream
5 egg whites

Sprinkle the gelatin over the rum or orange juice. Let stand 10 minutes. Melt the chocolate over hot water, with the milk. Heat until smooth. Add the gelatin and stir until melted. Pour into a bowl to cool.

Place the egg yolks and the sugar in top of the double boiler (do not bother to wash out the chocolate that remains). Beat together with a whisk or rotary beater until very thick and creamy, about 5 to 6 minutes. Do this over hot, but not boiling, water. Remove from the hot water and beat about 3 to 4 minutes to cool it off. Then add the vanilla and the chocolate mixture. Refrigerate until cold and partly set. Whip the cream and the egg whites separately. Beat into the partly set chocolate mixture. Make a waxed paper collar around a 3/4 quart (625 mL) straight-sided soufflé or baking dish that is suitable for serving. Pour mixture into dish.

Refrigerate 4 to 12 hours. Remove collar and sprinkle top and sides with icing sugar. Serves 6.

COLD STRAWBERRY SOUFFLÉ

Wonderful to serve all year round as it is made with frozen berries. It has a beautiful pale pink color, and is very attractive garnished with a few rose petals and green leaves.

1 envelope gelatin,
    unflavored
1/4 cup (60 mL) cold water
1 box frozen strawberries
4 egg yolks

1 cup (250 mL) sugar
1/2 tsp (2 mL) salt
1 cup (250 mL) whipping
    cream
4 egg whites

Soak the gelatin in the 1/4 cup (60 mL) cold water for 5 minutes.

Thaw out the strawberries and put through a sieve to make a purée. Mix together the egg yolks, 1/2 cup (125 mL) of the sugar and salt. Cook in double boiler, stirring almost constantly, until very light and creamy.

Remove from heat, add the gelatin. Cool and add the strawberries.

Beat the egg whites, add the second half cup (125 mL) of sugar, and beat until stiff.

Whip the cream, pour over the siffly beaten egg whites and fold into the strawberry mixture. Pour into a 2-quart (2 L) mold or soufflé dish. Keep refrigerated until ready to serve. Serves 8.

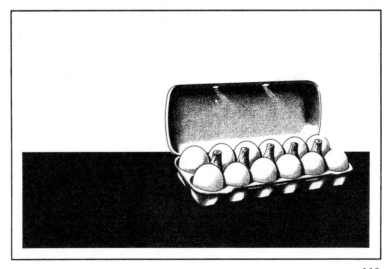

HONEY MOUSSE

A simple frozen mousse I learned to make while on a trip to New Orleans. The superb brandied apricot sauce that tops it is a cherished recipe of mine as I have used it on light cakes, bread pudding, and even plum pudding.

3/4 cup (190 mL) fine honey
juice and grated rind of 1
   lemon
4 eggs
2 cups (500 mL) whipping
   cream

1 tsp (5 mL) almond extract
1 large can apricots
1/4 cup (60 mL) brandy*
1/4 cup (60 mL) slivered
   almonds
1 tbsp (15 mL) butter

Heat the honey, lemon juice and rind in the top of a double boiler. Beat the eggs and, while beating, slowly pour the hot honey on top. Put back into double boiler and stir over boiling water until the mixture thickens. Pour into a dish and refrigerate until quite cold. Whip the cream and fold into honey mixture. Add the almond extract. Turn into freezing tray of refrigerator, and freeze until a 1-inch (2.5-cm) layer is frozen around the edges, about 1 hour.

Remove to a bowl and beat until smooth. Then freeze firm, about 1 to 1 1/2 hours. Remember that a mousse does not harden like ice cream, it retains its creamy light texture. Serves 8.

To make the sauce, pass the drained apricots through a sieve or whirl in a blender. Add the brandy and mix well. Brown the slivered almonds in the butter. Spread on a paper and set aside. Refrigerate the sauce. To serve, unmold the mousse which is easy if you dip the bottom of the pan in boiling water for a second. Add the toasted almonds to the apricot purée and pour over the mousse.

*Lemon juice may replace the brandy.

INDEX

Vegetables

Soups

Desserts

— NOTES —

— NOTES —

— NOTES —

— NOTES —

Printed by
PAYETTE & SIMMS, INC.
in May, 1988
at Saint-Lambert, Qué.